Un [W9-BAI-589]
Palestin... Israeli Conflic

01/2012

**PALM BEACH COUNTY**
**LIBRARY SYSTEM**
**3650 Summit Boulevard**
**West Palm Beach, FL 33406-4198**

*for Geoff Hartman*

# Understanding the
# Palestinian-Israeli Conflict

## A Primer

Phyllis Bennis

OLIVE
BRANCH
PRESS

An imprint of Interlink Publishing Group, Inc.
**www.interlinkbooks.com**

This edition first published in 2009 by

OLIVE BRANCH PRESS
An imprint of Interlink Publishing Group, Inc.
46 Crosby Street, Northampton, Massachusetts 01060
www.interlinkbooks.com

Text copyright © Phyllis Bennis 2007, 2009
All maps courtesy of PASSIA unless otherwise noted in the text

Published in association with TARI (Trans-Arab Research Institute, Inc.)
TARI provides scholarly studies oriented towards understanding the present
social, cultural, economic and political issues confronting Middle Eastern
societies. It provides a venue for interactive meetings between Middle
Eastern and international participants and provides focused research and
public venues to analyze, discuss and present alternative perspectives.

All rights reserved. No part of this publication may be reproduced, stored
in a retrieval system, or transmitted in any form or by any means,
electronic, mechanical, photocopying, recording or otherwise without
the prior permission of the publisher.

Library of Congress Cataloging-in-Publication Data
Bennis, Phyllis, 1951–
Understanding the Palestinian-Israeli conflict : a primer /
by Phyllis Bennis. —1st ed.
    p. cm.
ISBN 978-1-56656-685-8
1.  Arab-Israeli conflict. 2.  United States—Foreign relations—Middle
East. 3.  Middle East—Foreign relations—United States.
I. Title.
DS119.7.B38386 2007
956.9405′4—dc22

                                       2006100376

Cover image by George Azar

Printed and bound in the United States of America
10  9  8  7  6  5  4  3

To request our complete 48-page full-color catalog, please call us toll free
at 1-800-238-LINK, visit our website at www.interlinkbooks.com or write
Interlink Publishing, 46 Crosby Street, Northampton, MA 01060
e-mail: info@interlinkbooks.com

# CONTENTS

PART III——RECENT HISTORY: RISING VIOLENCE

—PART I—

THE CRISIS

### *Why is there so much violence in the Middle East? Isn't there violence on both sides?*

The violence in Israel and the occupied Palestinian territories has come from both sides. Its human tragedies are equally devastating for all victims and all their families. Innocents, including children, have been killed on and by both sides, and both sides have violated international law. But the violence by Israelis and by Palestinians is not an equal opportunity killer; it does not have the same roots, nor are the two sides culpable in the same way.

Palestinians in the territories live under Israeli military occupation. They are not citizens of Israel or of any state, and have no rights of protest or redress. The occupation is a violent daily reality, in which Israeli soldiers, checkpoints, tanks, helicopter gunships, and F-16 fighter jets control every aspect of Palestinian lives, and have recently brought social, family, and economic life to a virtual halt. In summer 2002, the US Agency for International Development determined that Palestinian children living in the occupied territories faced malnutrition at one of the highest levels in the world—higher than in Somalia and Bangladesh. By the summer of 2006, UN humanitarian agencies warned that poverty in Gaza was close to 80 percent, and unemployment over 40 percent. The occupation has been in place since 1967, although the current period has seen perhaps the most intense Israeli stranglehold on Palestinian life, and the highest levels of violence. What we often hear described simply as "the violence" in the Middle East cannot be understood without an understanding of what military occupation means.

Violence is central to maintaining Israel's military occupation. It is carried out primarily by Israeli military forces and Israeli settlers in the occupied territories who are themselves armed by the Israeli military, and its victims include some Palestinian militants and a large majority of Palestinian civilians, including many children. Because military occupation is itself illegal, all Israeli violence in the occupied territories stands in violation of international law— specifically the Geneva Conventions that identify the obligations of an occupying power to protect the occupied population.

Palestinian violence is the violence of resistance, and has escalated as conditions of life and loss of hope breed greater desperation. It is carried out primarily by individual Palestinians and those linked to small armed factions, and is aimed mostly at military checkpoints, soldiers, and settlers in the occupied territories; recently more attacks, particularly suicide bombings, have been launched inside Israel, many of which have targeted civilian gathering places. Those attacks, targeting civilians, are themselves a violation of international law. But the overall right of an occupied population to resist a foreign military occupation, including through use of arms against military targets, is recognized as lawful under international law.

*Why should we care about violence in the Middle East?*

When we learn about it, which is not always the case, we all tend to care about violence and its effects on people's lives wherever it may be. In the case of Israel and Palestine, the violence is on the front pages of our newspapers and a top story on radio and television on a daily basis. Many, all over the world, are particularly concerned about violence there because of the religious significance of the area—including historical sites holy to Judaism, Christianity, and Islam.

Beyond the general concern about human suffering, many Americans have a special interest in events in the region because the US government is by far the most dominant outside power there, and decisions made in Washington are central to developments toward war or peace. And further, the US sends billions of our tax dollars in aid to the region, including about $4 billion in annual aid to Israel alone.

US, British, and European policy in the Middle East also plays a major role in determining how people in that region view our governments and citizens. If we are concerned about the rise in international antagonism not only to US policies but toward individual citizens of our countries, we need to take seriously what our governments do in our name elsewhere in the world.

*Why is the Middle East so important to the US and internationally?*

From earliest history, the Middle East, and the area

long known as Palestine, were global crossroads of trade, science, scholarship, and religion in ancient civilizations. In more recent times, the discovery of oil in the region and the need of outside empires for reliable local allies led to the creation of western protectorates throughout the Middle East. As they struggle to rebuild after World World II, the European colonial powers long dominant in the Middle East lost much of their influence. France remained influential in Syria and Lebanon, but with the 1947 Partition Agreement in Palestine, Britain pulled back. Soon afterward, the US moved into the breach.

From 1967, through the beginnings of the twenty-first century, US policy in the region has been based on protecting the triad of oil, Israel, and stability. "Stability" has always been understood to include access to markets, raw materials, and labor forces for US business interests, as well as the stability imposed by the expansion of US military capacity throughout the region, including the creation of an elaborate network of US military bases. During the Cold War the US relied on Israel as a cat's paw—a military extension of its own strategic reach—both within the Middle East region and internationally in places as far as Angola, Guatemala, Mozambique, and Nicaragua. With the end of the Cold War, Israel remains a close and reliable ally, in the region as well as internationally, for the now unchallenged power of the US—although the strategic value of Israel, in an era shaped by the US's efforts to dominate countries and regions particularly antagonistic to Israel, appears to be diminishing. At the same time, widespread domestic support for Israel, most concentrated in the mainstream Jewish community and among the increasingly powerful right-wing Christian funda-mentalists in the US, took root in popular culture and politics, giving Israel's supporters great influence over Washington policymakers.

### What caused the Israeli–Palestinian crisis that began in 2000?

The crisis began in September 2000, after the Camp David summit had collapsed, and with it the hopes of Palestinians that the negotiations of the Oslo process would finally lead to an end to occupation and creation of an independent Palestinian state. The uprising, or "intifada" in Arabic, was sparked on September 27, 2000, by then Israeli Prime Minister Ariel Sharon's highly provocative decision to walk, accompanied by about 1,000 armed Israeli troops, on the Haram al-Sharif, or Noble Sanctuary, the Muslim holy site in East Jerusalem. (The complex is also known as the Temple Mount, the holiest site for religious Jews because the most sacred temple in Judaism was once located here—of which the Western, or Wailing, Wall, which borders the Haram al-Sharif, is believed to be a remnant.) The next day, Israeli troops opened fire on Palestinian protestors, some of whom were throwing stones, killing several Palestinians, some on the steps and inside the doorway of the al-Aqsa Mosque. What came to be called the "al-Aqsa Intifada" began that day.

### Why is the violence so intense?

Israel has increasingly escalated the weapons it deploys against the Palestinians. Numerous respected human rights organizations, including Amnesty International, Human Rights Watch, and Physicians for Human Rights have documented Israeli soldiers employing excessive force in their suppression of Palestinian demonstrators. Their reports cite the use of live ammunition against unarmed civilians, attacks on medical personnel and installations, the use of snipers with high-powered rifles, and attacks on children.

As the al-Aqsa Intifada ground on, Israel escalated to the use of tank-mounted weapons, helicopter gunships firing wire-guided missiles on buildings and streets to carry out targeted assassinations, and finally F-16 fighter bombers, which dropped 2,000-pound bombs in refugee camps and on crowded apartment buildings, resulting in significant civilian casualties.

Palestinians, unlike during the unarmed first intifada (1987–1993), had and used small arms, mainly rifles, against Israeli soldiers, tanks, and sometimes settlers; they also fired Qassam rockets that hit both military and civilian targets inside Israel. As the situation became more desperate, some young people turned themselves into suicide bombers, attacking either military checkpoints in the occupied territories, or civilian gathering spots inside Israel itself.

## Isn't Israel just trying to fight terrorism, as the US and the UK tried to do in Afghanistan?

Whether or not one believes going to war in Afghanistan was an appropriate response to the crime against humanity committed on September 11, 2001, it is a far different scenario than that faced by Israel.

Israel has every right to arrest and put on trial anyone attempting to attack civilians inside the country. But it does not have the right to occupy a neighboring country, and if it is serious about ending attacks on civilians, it must be serious about ending that occupation.

Israel is occupying Palestinian land and harshly controlling Palestinian lives; Palestinian violence, even those extreme and ultimately illegal actions such as lethal attacks on civilian targets, is a response to that occupation. Israel does not have the right, under international law or United Nations resolutions, to continue its occupation, let alone to use violent methods to enforce it.

Since September 11, Israeli politicians led by Prime Minister Ariel Sharon and his successor Ehud Olmert have ratcheted up their rhetoric equating the US "war on terrorism" in Afghanistan and later Iraq with Israeli assaults in the occupied Palestinian territories. Immediately after the September 11 attacks, former Prime Minister Benjamin Netanyahu blurted out, "It's very good." Then, editing his words, he added, "Well, not very good, but it will generate immediate sympathy."

Israel has also used the escalating fear of terrorism in the US after September 11 to increase its support (financial, diplomatic, and political) from Congress and the American people. In fact, the Bush administration's post-September 11 embrace of the extremist Sharon government has allowed new threats of even more dire Israeli attacks against Palestinians— up to and perhaps including forced "transfer" of Palestinians out of the occupied territories—to go unchallenged by Washington and to become part of normal political discourse inside Israel.

***Are all Palestinians terrorists or supporters of terrorism?***
The US State Department defines terrorism as: "premeditated, politically motivated violence perpetrated against noncombatant targets by sub-national groups or clandestine agents, usually intended to influence an audience." Under that definition, Palestinian attacks on civilians inside Israel would be considered terrorism; so would attacks on Palestinian marketplaces by Israeli settlers in Hebron or elsewhere. Palestinian attacks on Israeli soldiers, military checkpoints, or other military targets would not fall under the definition of "terrorism," although many US politicians and pundits describe them as such.

The vast majority of Palestinians have never participated in any armed attack against anyone. Many, perhaps most, Palestinians are opposed to attacks on civilians anywhere, and many are opposed to any attacks inside Israel. In the spring of 2002, a large group of well-known Palestinian intellectuals signed a public statement condemning suicide bombings against civilians. But virtually all Palestinians understand the desperation and hopelessness that fuel the rage of suicide bombers and their increasing (and ever-younger) followers.

### Why are Palestinians in Israel at all?

When Israel was created as a state in 1948, 750,000 indigenous Palestinians, whose families had lived in Palestine for hundreds of years, were forcibly expelled by, or fled in terror of, the powerful militias that would soon become the army of the State of Israel. The one million or so Palestinians inside Israel today, who constitute just under 20 percent of the Israeli population, are those that remained and their descendants. Despite international law and specific UN resolutions, none of those forced into exile have been allowed to return. In fact, Israel's admission to the UN in 1948 was conditioned on its willingness to abide by General Assembly Resolution 194 calling for the right to return and compensation.

From Israel's creation in 1948 until 1966, the indigenous Palestinian population inside the country lived under military rule. Since that time, Palestinians have been considered citizens, can vote and run for office; several Palestinians serve in the Israeli Knesset, or parliament. But not all rights inside Israel are granted on the basis of citizenship. Some rights and obligations, sometimes known as "nationality rights," favor Jews over non-Jews (who are overwhelmingly Palestinian) in social services, the right to own land, access to bank loans and education, military service, and more.

More than three times as many Palestinians live under Israeli military occupation in the West Bank, Gaza, and East Jerusalem than remain inside Israel proper. Millions more remain refugees.

***Who are the Palestinians? Where did they come from?***
Palestinian Arabs are descendants of the indigenous people of Palestine, who lived under the vast Arab/Islamic empire that from the seventh century dominated Palestine, during the rise of the Arabic language and Arab/Islamic culture. While the majority of Palestinians were peasants, Palestinian cities, especially Jerusalem, were hubs of Arab civilization, where scholars, poets, and scientists congregated and where, enriched by a constant influx of traders, they forged the city's identity as an important national center. Islam's religious and moral teachings remained the dominant social forces, but small indigenous Jewish communities remained as integral parts of the Palestinian community. They were the remnants of Palestine's ancient Jewish kingdom, which was conquered by Rome in 70 CE, its people largely scattered. Along with groups of Christians, those Palestinian Jews maintained their faith and separate communal identities within broader Palestinian society throughout the rise of Islam.

Throughout the years of the Arab and then Ottoman empires in what is now the Arab world, there were no nation-states; instead the political demography was shaped by cities and regions. As in most parts of the Arab world, modern national consciousness for Palestinians grew in the context of demographic changes and shifts in colonial control. During the 400 years of Ottoman Turkish control, Palestine was a distinct and identifiable region within the larger empire, but linked closely with the region then known as Greater Syria. With World War I and the defeat of the Ottoman Empire, Palestine became part of the British Empire. But even before that, beginning in the 1880s, the increasing influx of European Jewish settlers brought about a new national identity—a distinctly Palestinian consciousness—among the Muslims and Christians who were the overwhelming majority of Palestinian society. The indigenous Palestinians— Muslims and Christians—fought the colonial ambitions of European Jewish settlers, British colonial rule during the inter-war period, and the Israeli occupation since 1948 and 1967.

### What are the occupied territories?

When the British ended their Palestine Mandate in 1947, they turned control over to the United Nations. The UN Partition Agreement of November 29, 1947, divided Palestine into sectors: 55 percent for a Jewish state and 45 percent for a Palestinian Arab state, with Jerusalem to be left under international control as a "corpus separatum" (separate body). War broke out immediately. After the 1947–1948 war, the new state of Israel was announced

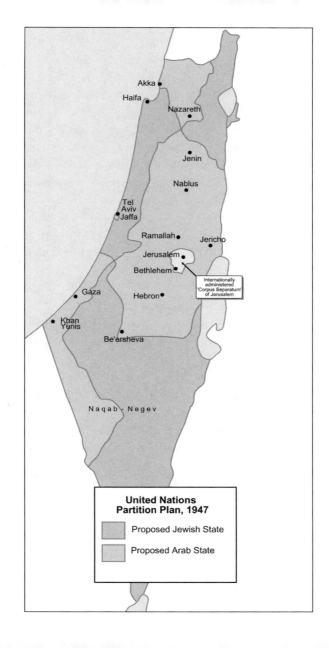

Akka
Haifa
Nazareth
Jenin
Nablus
Tel
Aviv
Jaffa
Ramallah
Jericho
Jerusalem
Bethlehem

Internationally
administered
'Corpus Separatum'
of Jerusalem

Gáza
Hebron
Khan
Yunis
Be'ersheva

N a q a b - N e g e v

**United Nations
Partition Plan, 1947**

Proposed Jewish State

Proposed Arab State

in June 1948, made up of 78 percent of the land of what had been British Mandate Palestine under the League of Nations since 1922. Only 22 percent was left, made up of the Gaza Strip (a small piece of land along the Mediterranean coast abutting the Egyptian border), the West Bank, along the Jordan River, and Arab East Jerusalem. From 1948 until the June War of 1967, the Gaza Strip was controlled by Egypt; the West Bank and East Jerusalem were governed by Jordan.

In the 1967 war, Israel took over the West Bank, Gaza, and East Jerusalem, the last 22 percent of historic Palestine. Those areas are now identified as the occupied territories.

### What does "military occupation" mean?

Military occupation means complete Israeli control over every facet of Palestinian civil and economic life. Israel has regularly closed its borders to the more than 125,000 Palestinian workers—primarily from Gaza—who rely on hardscrabble jobs inside Israel for their still-insufficient income. Just from October 2000 through September 2001, the UN estimated that Palestinian workers lost between $2.4 and $3.2 billion in income due to closures. In April 2002, unemployment estimates from the World Bank and others were at 50 percent and rising across the Palestinian territories.

During the second intifada, settlement construction and expansion escalated. The curfews and closures, or blockades, of Palestinian towns and cities, once an occasional disruption, became constant. The re-occupation of Palestinian cities was matched by a complete division of the West Bank into scores of tiny cantons—villages cut off from each other, small towns cut off from the main roads, cities surrounded as in medieval sieges. Armed checkpoints, huge earth berms dug by armored tractors, destruction of roads, all served to prevent Palestinians from moving within the territories, let alone traveling into Israel. Inevitably the economic shortages were severe; truckloads of produce rotted in the sun at checkpoints, milk soured, workers could not get to their jobs. Humanitarian crises spiked, with women giving birth at checkpoints because soldiers would not allow them to pass, victims of settler or soldier violence dying because military officers would not authorize Palestinian ambulances to move. In June 2006, the World Food Program reported that 70 percent of the Gaza population were unable to cover their daily food needs without outside assistance.

Israeli military control also means complete dependence on Israel for permits—to travel out of the country, to enter Israel from the West Bank to get to the airport to leave the country, for a doctor to move from her home village to her clinic in town, for a student to go to school. Most of the time, these permits remain out of reach.

In the summer of 2005, Israel withdrew its soldiers and settlers from the territory of the Gaza Strip. But that did not end the occupation, because international law defines occupation as the control of territory by an outside force. In the case of Gaza, after the "disengagement" of troops and settlers, Israel remained in complete control of Gaza's borders, the entry and exit of goods and people, Gaza's airspace, the sea off Gaza's coast. Israel prohibited the rebuilding of the Gaza airport, which it had destroyed in 2000, and prevented the construction of a seaport.

### Who are the Israelis? Where did they come from?

Israel defines itself as a state of and for the Jewish people, and about 80 percent of the population are Jews. It is, however, a country of immigrants, and unlike the indigenous Palestinian Israelis, the vast majority of Jewish Israelis (or their ancestors) have come to Israel from all over the world in the last 120 years, but mostly since 1948. The tiny indigenous and intensely orthodox Jewish communities in places like Safed and Jerusalem have largely remained separate from the mainstream or even the "regular" ultra-orthodox Israeli Jewish population.

The Israeli Jewish community is roughly divided into Ashkenazi, or European, Jews—of whom about one-fifth are Russians who arrived in the 1990s—and Mizrachi Jews. The Mizrachim constitute a wide-ranging category, usually including Jews from Africa and Asia as well as Spain and Latin America. But the majority of the Mizrachim are Arab—they or their forebears emigrated to Israel from Morocco, Yemen, Syria, Egypt, or other Arab countries—or Turkish, Persian, Kurdish, or from elsewhere in the Middle East. Historically there has been significant tension within Israel between Jews of European descent and those whose ancestors come from the Arab world, since Israeli society is heavily racialized and has tended to privilege the Europeans.

About nineteen percent of Israeli citizens are Muslim or Christian Palestinian Arabs.

It was European and Russian Jews, back in the 1880s, who first began significant Jewish immigration to what was then Ottoman Turkish- and later British-ruled Palestine. They came fleeing persecution and violent pogroms, or communal attacks, in czarist Russia and eastern Europe, and they came in answer to mobilizations organized by a movement known as Zionism, which called for all Jews to leave their countries of origin to live in a Jewish state they wanted to create in Palestine. The use of Hebrew, re-created as a modern language in the late 1800s, an orientation toward and identification with Europe and the US rather than the neighboring Middle Eastern countries, and nearly universal military service (excepting only Arabs and ultra-orthodox Jews) became the central anchors around which national consciousness was built.

Israel defines itself as a state of the entire Jewish people, wherever they live, not simply a state for its own citizens. It encourages Jewish immigration through what is known as the Law of Return, under which any Jew born anywhere in the world, with or without pre-existing ties to Israel, has the official right to claim immediate citizenship upon arrival in Israel, and the right to all the privileges of being Jewish in a Jewish state—including state-financed language classes, housing, job placement, medical and welfare benefits, etc. Only Jews automatically have the right to immigrate to Israel; the indigenous Palestinians and their descendants, including those expelled from their homeland in 1947–1948 and 1967, are denied that right, despite the guarantees of UN Resolution 194 (institutionalizing the Palestinian right of return) and those of the Universal Declaration on Human Rights.

### What's the difference between Jews and Israelis?

Technically Jews are a religious grouping; in the real world Jews are defined by a complex web of religious, cultural, ethnic, and other communal ties. Israelis are Israeli citizens, including Palestinian citizens of Israel.

Language often gets confusing, and is often used in sloppy ways, both internationally and within Israel itself, where the term "Jews" is often used inter-changeably with "Israelis" or sometimes "settlers." As a result, Palestinians in the occupied territories often fall into the same habit of conflating the terms.

### Who are the Israeli settlers? Why are the Israeli settlements located outside Israel's borders?

Immediately after the 1967 war, some extremist Israelis moved to establish Jewish colonies in the newly occupied territories. The first, created in Hebron in 1968, was led by American-born Rabbi Meir Kahane and sanctioned by a Labor Party government. Israeli governments have justified construction of the settlements both for security and ideological reasons.

The Labor Party, committed to Israeli military control of all land west of the Jordan River, justified settlements in the name of security. The right-wing Likud Bloc supported settlements to assert its claim of Jewish sovereignty over the entire Biblical-era "Greater Israel," and when a Likud government won power in 1977, settlement construction expanded dramatically.

As settler expansion increased, religious and nationalist extremists became a minority among the settlers themselves. Most moved to settlements in the occupied territories because government stipends keep mortgages low, amenities accessible, and commuting to jobs inside Israel easy because of a network of settler-only roads known as "bypass roads," designed to connect settlements to each other and to Israel without traversing Palestinian towns.

Since 1993, when the Oslo "peace process" began, the settler population has nearly doubled. More than 400,000 Israeli Jewish settlers now live in the occupied territories, 200,000 of them in Arab East Jerusalem. The Jerusalem settlers are particularly problematic, since Israel annexed East Jerusalem after the 1967 war, and while that annexation is not recognized by any other government or the UN, many Israelis deny that East Jerusalem is occupied territory at all.

Settler expansion has continued under both Labor- and Likud-led governments. Although Israeli governments have often tried to distinguish between "authorized" and "unauthorized" settlements (distinguishing those officially authorized by the government), in fact all the settlements are in violation of international law. Article 49 of the Fourth Geneva Convention specifically prohibits an occupying power from transferring any part of its own civilian population into the territory it occupies. In fact, international humanitarian law prohibits any permanent change to an occupied land, including imposed demographic changes, that are not intended to benefit the local (occupied) population.

US administrations have identified the settlements variously as "illegal," as "obstacles to peace," and as "unhelpful." But they have consistently accepted Israel's distinctions between "authorized" and "unauthorized" settlements, calling for the dismantling (and rarely even that) only of the "unauthorized" settlements, as if the older, huge settlement blocs were somehow legal. President George W. Bush called for a settlement freeze in his speech on Middle East policy in April 2002, but has foresworn identifying the settlements as illegal or doing anything to encourage Israel to eliminate the settlements and return the settlers to homes inside Israel.

### What do the Palestinians want?

Many Palestinians, those in their sixties or older, remember being expelled from their homes inside what is now Israel but what was then Palestine, in 1947 or '48. Some of them, though now growing old, still hold the keys to their homes that they kept as they fled, thinking they would be back in days or weeks. Many more remember the terror of being expelled from their homes in the West Bank and Gaza in 1967, finding minimal shelter in refugee camps that became home for nearly 40. Palestinians want dignity, human rights, equality, and a state of their own.

In 1988, in an enormous, historic compromise, the Palestinian National Council, or parliament-in-exile, voted to accept a two-state solution that would return to Palestinians only the 22 percent of their land that had been occupied in 1967. They accepted that the other 78 percent would remain Israel. While some individual Palestinians and some smaller organizations still reject that historic compromise, for the vast majority of Palestinians the goal is an independent state—a fully realized and truly independent, sovereign, and viable state—encompassing all of the West Bank and Gaza, with East Jerusalem as its capital.

Palestinians also insist on the internationally guaranteed right for refugees to return to the homes from which they were expelled. The right of return is part of international law, and Palestinians are specifically guaranteed that right by UN Resolution 194, which states that "refugees wishing to return to their homes and live at peace with their neighbors should be permitted to do so at the earliest practicable date, and that compensation should be paid for the property of those choosing not to return."

Simply calling for "an end to the violence" is insufficient, because it would leave in place the structures of military occupation that prevent Palestinians from realizing their full national rights and their human rights to dignity, equality, and independence.

### What does Israel want?

Most Jewish Israelis want to live their lives very much as they have been doing for the last decade or so, but with an end to the occupation-driven attacks on civilians that have brought such fear to ordinary Israelis. Until its recent economic downturn, Israel had been the seventeenth wealthiest country in the world, with a high standard of living and close ties to Europe and the US.

Only a minority of Israelis, according to the polls, are committed to holding on to the occupied territories, but the majority, willing to return the territories to the Palestinians and end the occupation, has not been able to influence Israel's successive governments to do just that. Since the intifada began in September 2000, many Israelis have taken up the view that Palestinian violence can somehow be quashed by ever-increasing use of force, while leaving the occupation intact. Despite its failure so far, a majority still seem to accept or support that position. In the aftermath of the summer 2006 war in Lebanon, the number of Israelis prepared to even consider withdrawal from any part of the West Bank has diminished.

For most Israelis, an end to Palestinian resistance violence would be sufficient, regardless of whether the occupation remained intact.

### Who controls the West Bank, East Jerusalem, and the Gaza Strip?

Israel occupied those areas in the 1967 Six-Day War,

and imposed military control of all of them through checkpoints, soldiers, and weapons. The 1993 Oslo peace process brought about a division of the West Bank into "A, B, and C" areas. The B areas (over 400 Palestinian villages), which amounted to 23 percent of the West Bank, and the C areas, 70 percent of the land (including Israeli settlements, army camps, and state-seized land that used to be cultivated by Palestinian farmers), remained officially under Israeli control. A areas (the cities), which amounted to only about three percent of the West Bank, were ostensibly placed under Palestinian security control. But the Palestinian-controlled areas were tiny islands surrounded by roads and lands that remained under direct Israeli military occupation. In 2002, during the Palestinian uprising, Israel moved to re-occupy all but one of the major cities that were supposed to be under Palestinian control, and moved to tighten complete Israeli control of the roads, bridges, and agricultural land throughout the West Bank.

The 2002 re-occupation of the cities made clear that Oslo's version of Palestinian "control" was incomplete and thoroughly reversible; Israeli military occupation remained in place, controlling the land and the lives of Palestinians, Israel remains in control of the economic life of Palestine through road and town closures and border controls, and by imposing a complete economic embargo on the Palestinians beginning in January 2006. Israel controls Palestinian political life by preventing the Oslo-created Palestinian

Authority from meeting, keeping PA officials from meeting or carrying out their responsibilities, and ensuring the PA has no actual power. It controls social life through checkpoints separating cities and villages; by separating families and denying residency permits both in Jerusalem and in the West Bank and Gaza; by denying access to Jerusalem's, Bethlehem's, and Hebron's Muslim and Christian shrines; by preventing access to health and educational institutions, and more.

### Why does Israel still occupy those areas?

The first settlers after the 1967 war established settlements as part of asserting Israeli Jewish control over all of Palestine, which they called "Eretz Israel," or the "Land of Israel." Later settlers, and the governments that supported them, claimed the settlements, especially those in the Jordan Valley, played a vital role in protecting Israel from possible attack from Arab states to the east.

In the 1990s "yuppie settlers," uninterested in nationalist or religious rationales and concerned only with the amenities of settler life, became the majority; most indicated they would be willing to give up their homes if they were properly compensated. But increasingly, the minority of ideologically driven settlers, both religious and nationalist extremists, became far more powerful than their numbers, especially within the ranks of the right-wing Likud Bloc. Holding on to the settlements, even the most isolated, became an article of faith and a domestic political necessity for one Israeli government after another. Likud leader General Ariel Sharon himself, speaking before the 2005 Gaza "disengagement," described Netzarim, a tiny isolated settlement in Gaza, as "the same as Tel Aviv" in importance.

Beyond the politics and the hyperbolic claims of military protection (irrelevant in an era of rockets), the settlements do play one important role in Israeli national life. They allow the diversion of almost all of the West Bank water sources, its underground aquifers, to Israeli settlements and ultimately into Israel itself. Indigenous Palestinians, farmers on parched land and villagers with insufficient water pressure even for a household tap, pay the price for that diversion of water, even as they watch the settlements' sparkling swimming pools and verdant, sprinkler-watered lawns.

### If Jerusalem is the capital of Israel, why are there so many Palestinians in the eastern part of the city?

During the 1948 war, the Israeli military conquered only the western half of the city, most of which was still owned by Palestinian Arabs, and declared it the capital of Israel. East Jerusalem remained virtually entirely Palestinian, with the exception of a handful of religious Jews who remained in the Old City's ancient Jewish Quarter, during the city's 1948–1967 years under Jordanian administration. In those years, Israeli Jews were prohibited from entering East Jerusalem, and Palestinians were kept out of West Jerusalem. In

1967, when the Israeli army conquered East Jerusalem along with the West Bank, Gaza Strip, the Syrian Golan Heights, and Egypt's Sinai Peninsula, one of Israel's first acts was to declare Jerusalem an eternally "united" city. In fact it was never unified; the old border, or Green Line, was legally erased, but remained vivid in the minds of Jerusalemites on both sides. During the first Palestinian intifada, or uprising, from 1987–1993, which pitted unarmed stone-throwing children and youths against the Israeli occupation forces, taxi drivers from West Jerusalem would routinely refuse to take passengers into the eastern part of the city, claiming they or their passengers would be at risk.

But immediately after the 1967 occupation, Israel began building huge settlements blocs within East Jerusalem, such as French Hill and Pisagot, which were quickly incorporated into Jewish Jerusalem and never acknowledged as settlements. There are now 200,000 Israeli Jews living in East Jerusalem settlements primly defined as "neighborhoods."

Simultaneously, Palestinian Jerusalemites found their rights severely constrained. Permits for building new houses or additions to over-crowded homes were and remain virtually unobtainable for Palestinians. Marrying a partner from outside the city can put one's residency permit at risk. Palestinian Arabs in East Jerusalem are considered legal residents of the city—thus they have the right to vote for city council—but are denied full Israeli citizenship.

### *Who are the Palestinian refugees and why are they still living in refugee camps?*

There are two categories of Palestinian refugees. The first wave, about 750,000 at the time, were expelled by force or driven out by fear before, during, and after the 1947–48 hostilities. Some were physically driven out, others heard stories of massacres, such as that at the village of Deir Yassin outside of Jerusalem, in April 1948, in which 254 Palestinian civilians were killed by soldiers from the pre-state Zionist militias. Following the massacre, soldiers drove trucks through other Palestinian villages using loudspeakers to threaten "Deir Yassin, Deir Yassin!" in a kind of psychological warfare warning to any Palestinians who remained. Many fled the campaign of ethnic cleansing, believing the onslaught by the Zionist militias would end within a few weeks and they would return home. Of those, many carried with them the keys to their houses, believing their return was imminent, and thus the key has become a symbol of Palestinian refugee rights. Many of that aging first generation of refugees are still alive, living in refugee camps or in exile with their children and grand-children, clinging to the keys and the hope that they will be allowed to go home before they die.

For many years Israeli officials and many defenders of Israel claimed that the Palestinians who left did so only because they were ordered to by Arab leaders broadcasting on local radio, who allegedly promised them they would be able to return

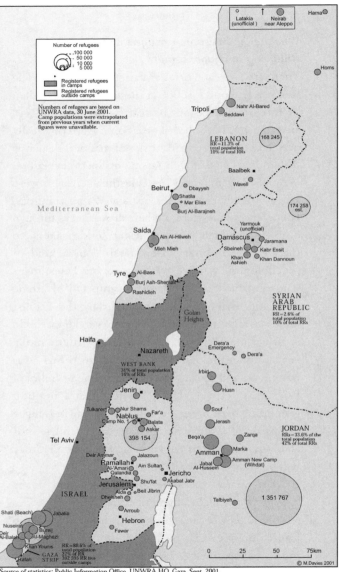

Number of refugees
- 100 000
- 50 000
- 10 000
- 5 000

Registered refugees in camps
Registered refugees outside camps

Numbers of refugees are based on UNWRA data, 30 June 2001. Camp populations were extrapolated from previous years when current figures were unavailable.

Latakia (unofficial)    Neirab near Aleppo    Hama

Homs

Tripoli    Nahr Al-Bared
Beddawi

LEBANON
RR = 11.3% of total population
10% of total RRs    168 245

Baalbek    Wavell

Beirut    Dbayyeh
Shatila
Mar Elias
Burj Al-Barajneh    174 258 est.

Mediterranean Sea

Yarmouk (unofficial)

Saida    Ain Al-Hilweh    Damascus    Jaramana
Sbeineh    Kabr Essit
Mieh Mieh    Khan    Khan Dannoun
Ashieh

Tyre    Al-Bass
Burj Ash-Shemali
Rashidieh    SYRIAN ARAB REPUBLIC
RR = 2.6% of total population
10% of total RRs

Golan Heights

Haifa    Dera'a Emergency    Dera'a

Nazareth    Irbid

WEST BANK
31% of total population
16% of RRs    Husn

Jenin    Souf

Tulkarem    Nur Shams    Far'a    Jerash
Nablus    Camp No. 1    Balata
Askar    Beqa'a    Zarqa    JORDAN
RRs = 33.6% of the total population
42% of total RRs

Tel Aviv    398 154    Amman    Marka
Deir Ammar    Jalazoun    Jabal    Amman New Camp
Ramallah    Ain Sultan    Al-Hussein    (Wihdat)
Al-'Amari    Jericho
Qalandia    Akabat Jabr
Jerusalem    Shu'fat
Aida    Beit Jibrin
ISRAEL    Dheisheh    Talbiyeh    1 351 767
Arroub
Shati (Beach)    Jabalia    Hebron
Nuseirat    Bureij    Fawar
Deir    Al-Maghazi
Al-Balah
Khan Younis
Rafah    GAZA STRIP    RR = 80.6% of total population
22% of RR
392 595 RR live outside camps

0    25    50    75km

© M.Davies 2001

Source of statistics: Public Information Office, UNWRA HQ, Gaza, Sept. 2001.

• 28 •

victorious. But throughout the 1990s, an increasingly large number of Israeli academics, the "new historians," carefully researched and completely debunked that myth. There were no such radio broadcasts. Some of the civilians fled because they were attacked by the Haganah, Palmach, and Irgun militias. Others fled in fear and believed they would eventually be able to come home because it is a longstanding tenet of international law that war-time refugees, regardless of the particular circumstances under which they flee, have the right to return home.

When Palestinians were expelled from their homes in the 1948 war, many fled to neighboring Arab countries, others to the West Bank and Gaza Strip, the parts of Palestine not yet under the control of the new Israeli army. In all those places, corrupt and/or impoverished Arab governments had neither the will nor the resources to care for the sudden influx of refugees. The United Nations, recognizing its responsibility for the crisis through its role in dividing Palestine in the first place, took on the work of caring for the new exiles. It created the United Nations Relief and Work Agency (UNRWA), designed to provide basic housing, food, medical care, and education to the Palestinian refugees until they could return home; UNRWA was initially envisioned as a short-term project. But Israel refused to allow the refugees to return home. Instead, the months turned to years, and tent camps were transformed over time into squalid, crowded mini-towns, made up of concrete block houses with tin roofs held down by old tires and sometimes scraps of iron bars. Electricity remains sporadic, and streams of raw sewage are a common feature between tightly packed houses. But UNRWA schools educated Palestinian children to such an extent that Palestinians today have the highest percentage of college-educated people in the entire Arab world.

Some have claimed that Arab governments have used Palestinian refugees to score propaganda points, or to divert their own people's anger away from the regimes and toward Israel. Certainly the Arab regimes had little interest in serious political defense of Palestinian rights, let alone serious protection of Palestinian refugees. Only Jordan allowed Palestinians to become citizens. Everywhere else, Palestinians were kept segregated. In Lebanon, they were viewed as a potential disruption to the country's delicate confessional system balancing Christians and Muslims, and well into the twenty-first century Palestinian refugees in Lebanon remain locked out of dozens of job categories. Egypt kept the Palestinians confined to the Gaza Strip.

But the refugee camps remained in place primarily because Israel blocked the refugees' right of return, and the Palestinians themselves were determined that they wanted to go home—they did not want to be "integrated" into other Arab countries, despite the common language. Palestinians were—and remain—afraid that leaving the camps to integrate into some other part of the Arab world would result in the loss of their homes and their rights. The Arab world after 1948 was no longer an integrated "Arabia": nation-states had been created by lines drawn in the sand by colonial powers, as in so many other places in the world. National ties combined with ties to a village or town to create for Palestinians a communal yearning to return home.

At the same time that the United Nations created UNRWA in 1948, it passed Resolution 194, which went beyond customary international law protecting all refugees to provide special protection for the Palestinians. The resolution reaffirmed that Palestinian "refugees wishing to return to their homes and live at peace with their neighbors should be permitted to do so at the earliest practicable date, and that compensation should be paid for the property of those choosing not to return." The UN even made Israel's own entry to the world body contingent on Israeli acceptance of Resolution 194.

When the West Bank and Gaza were occupied in 1967, many of those living there fled the fighting again, and were made refugees for a second time, finding homes in already overcrowded refugee camps in Lebanon, Jordan, and Syria. There was discussion at the 2000 Camp David summit about allowing some of the 1967 refugees to return to their homes in a future Palestinian state, but no consideration of the right of the refugees who so chose to return to their homes in what is now Israel. Ultimately there was no resolution. (Israel would remain in control of Palestine's borders, determining who would or would not be allowed to enter the ostensibly "independent" country.)

The 1948 refugees and their descendents, now numbering about five million worldwide, have the right under international law to return to their homes inside what is now Israel. But despite international law and the specific requirements of Resolution 194, Israel has never allowed Palestinian refugees to return to their homes. Israel maintains that allowing the Palestinian refugees to return would change its demographic balance, more than doubling Israel's current 19 percent Palestinian population. Israelis sometimes use the expression "demographic bomb" to describe the effect of large-scale immigration of Palestinians to Israel. However, international law does not allow a country to violate UN resolutions and international principles in order to protect its ethnic or religious composition. The parallel would be if Rwanda's new Tutsi-dominated government, after the 1994 genocide, announced that they would not allow the overwhelmingly Hutu refugees who fled during the war to return home, because it would disrupt the new ethnic balance in their country. The United Nations and the world, appropriately, would have made very clear that such a prohibition was unacceptable and that the refugees had to be allowed to return home. Palestinian refugees, despite the passage of time, have the same rights as their Rwandan counterparts.

Most Palestinians recognize that while rights, including the right of return, are absolute, how to implement rights can always be discussed. It is likely that once their right to return has been recognized, some Palestinian refugees may choose options other than permanent return to their mostly demolished villages in what is now Israel. But the key factor will be the ability of individual Palestinians to choose for themselves what to do. Some may choose to go home; some may wish to go only for short visits; some may wish to accept compensation and build new lives in a new Palestinian state; many may choose to accept compensation and citizenship in their place of refuge or in third countries. Some, especially among the most impoverished and disempowered Palestinian refugees living in Lebanon, may indeed choose to return to their homes in Israel. But discussion of how to implement this right of return (in a way that creates the least, rather than the greatest, disruption to Israeli society) cannot begin until Israel acknowledges its responsibility for the refugee crisis, and recognizes the internationally guaranteed right of return as an absolute right.

### What is the Palestine Liberation Organization (PLO)?

In 1964, the PLO was created and largely controlled by leaders of the Arab states. At the same time, small groups of Palestinian activists were building nationalist organizations, some of which, the *fedayeen*, moved toward guerrilla tactics to challenge Israel. In 1968, Yasir Arafat became head of the PLO, uniting a number of factions that advocated a wide range of tactics and political principles. The organization was cobbled together, with a complicated web of eight separate political factions represented in the leadership; a broadly representative parliament-in-exile, the

Palestine National Council; and a host of sector-based institutions including students' and women's unions, medical and relief agencies, and more. In many Palestinian-populated areas, particularly in Jordan and then in Lebanon, the PLO took on the responsibilities, and often the trappings, of a full government.

In the early years the PLO demanded a democratic secular state in all of Palestine—including what was now Israel as well as the 1967 occupied territories. There was no recognition of Israel having the right to exist as a separate Jewish state. But as the shock of the 1967 war and the resulting occupation began to wear off, Palestinians began to broaden their strategic approach. By the mid-'70s, the majority view in the PLO was moving toward acceptance of a two-state solution, an approach already accepted in the UN and elsewhere as reflecting an international consensus. In Israel, where refusal even to consider negotiations with the PLO was the norm, such a shift was viewed as potentially damaging, as it stripped away the key rationale for Israeli antagonism towards all Palestinian claims.

In 1974, the United Nations General Assembly recognized the PLO as the "sole legitimate representative of the Palestinian people." It established November 29 (the day the original partition resolution was signed in 1947) as an International Day of Solidarity with the Palestinian People, and invited the PLO to participate as an observer within the General Assembly and other UN agencies.

In January 1976, a PLO-drafted resolution backed by a number of Arab countries as well as the Soviet Union was put before the UN Security Council. It called for a two-state solution, Israeli withdrawal to the 1967 borders, and other aspects of the international consensus. Israel refused to participate in the meeting, and the US cast its veto, killing the resolution.

In 1982, the PLO led the joint Lebanese-Palestinian resistance to the Israeli invasion of Lebanon and weeks-long bombardment of Beirut. Soon after, diplomatic efforts led to the organization's expulsion from Lebanon, with thousands of PLO activists and fighters boarding ships to a new, long exile in Tunis.

Still, the two-state approach remained the majority view within the PLO for some years. In 1988, at the height of the first intifada, it became official when the Palestine National Council convened in Algiers. In a unanimous vote, the PNC proclaimed the "establishment of the State of Palestine on our Palestinian territory with its capital Jerusalem." Within the political program was official recognition of the two-state approach, despite the fact that the PLO was still an outlawed "terrorist" organization to Israel, and PLO officials were prohibited from even visiting Israel or the occupied territories.

The US opened mid-level diplomatic ties with the PLO a month later, but the organization remained excluded from the US-led international diplomatic efforts. With the Iraqi invasion of Kuwait in 1990, the PLO's decision to side with Iraq resulted in intense anger from the oil-rich Gulf countries that had long bankrolled the organization. Palestinians were summarily expelled from Saudi Arabia, Kuwait, and other Gulf states, and the PLO fell into severe poverty and political isolation in the region.

After the Gulf War, with the PLO at perhaps its weakest point, the US government, flush with its victory over Iraq, approached the PLO to negotiate Palestinian participation in the post-war peace talks in Madrid. The terms were dire—no separate Palestinian delegation, participation only as a sub-set of the Jordanian team, no participation for PLO members, no participation for Palestinian residents of Jerusalem, no role for the United Nations—and the PNC vote approving participation in the Madrid process was bitterly contested. But eventually, the PLO, through its well-known but officially unacknowledged representatives in the occupied territories, accepted. The talks, ostensibly based on UN Resolutions 242 and 338 and the principle of "land for peace," ground on uneventfully for almost two years, when the surprise announcement hit the press that secret Israeli—PLO talks had been underway in Oslo, and that a Declaration of Principles was about to be signed.

The ceremony on the White House lawn on September 13, 1993, in which President Clinton presided over a handshake between a reluctant Yitzhak Rabin and an eager Yasir Arafat, provided a photo-op of global proportions. A Nobel Prize for Peace, split between Arafat, Rabin, and the Israeli Foreign Minister Shimon

Peres, soon followed. The Oslo peace process was born.

Within two years and after extensive negotiations, Oslo's substantive agreements were signed; their crucial beginnings allowed the return of all the PLO exiles from Tunis to the West Bank and Gaza, where they would be allowed to create a new Palestinian Authority to administer small parts of the still-occupied territories under overall Israeli "security" control.

### What is the Palestinian Authority (PA)?

The PA was created under the terms of the Oslo peace process. It is a quasi-governmental body, with derivative power limited to what is granted to it (or taken away from it) by Israel. It is not a fully independent government, even in the limited areas under its jurisdiction from which Israeli troops have temporarily withdrawn, but rather analogous to a municipal council, with carefully delimited authority. It has the authority, in most Palestinian towns and cities, to orchestrate day-to-day life for residents, but not to control the land. It is responsible for running the schools and hospitals, cleaning the streets, and keeping economic and social life functioning, but it is denied the authority to control its own borders; it does not have any authority over Israeli soldiers or settlers within or surrounding its land; it does not control a single contiguous territory but rather scores of tiny scattered and disconnected areas; and, according to the language of the Oslo agreements, any law passed by the PA's parliament is subject to approval or rejection by Israel.

Beginning in the spring of 2002, as the intifada escalated, Israel moved to re-occupy almost all of Palestine's major cities, from which its troops had been withdrawn under the terms of Oslo. While Palestinian resistance was fierce in one or two of the cities (Jenin and Nablus in particular), the speed of the Israeli military's return gave the lie to any notion that Palestinian control, even partial, was designed to be permanent.

Following the withdrawal of Israeli soldiers and settlers from the territory of the Gaza Strip in 2005, the PA was assumed to have full control over Gaza. But Israeli control of Gaza's borders, as well as Gaza's entry and exit points, and the lack of any viable connection between Gaza and the West Bank made a mockery of PA authority. After the January 2005 elections, when the Islamist Hamas organization won majority control of the PA, the US and Israel orchestrated a global economic boycott of the PA that made it impossible to govern. By the summer of 2006, with Israel routinely bombing and attacking Gaza's infrastructure and carrying out "targeted assassinations," the Israeli military had arrested more than 40 members of the PA's legislature and about eight members of the cabinet; other PA officials went into hiding or on the run, undermining further any capacity to govern.

### Who are the "suicide bombers" and why are they killing themselves and others?

The intifada, or uprising, that began in September 2000 has seen the rise of a new phenomenon in

Palestinian resistance—suicide bombings. These are attacks in which a young man or woman straps explosives around their body, and detonates the charge in a public place, killing themselves and often killing and injuring many people nearby.

Islamist organizations such as Hamas and Islamic Jihad, which have often (though not always) opposed Palestinian diplomatic efforts, have claimed responsibility for most of the suicide bombings. Beginning in early 2002, the secular al-Aqsa Martyrs' Brigade, which is linked to the mainstream Fatah organization led by Yasir Arafat, began a suicide bombing campaign inside Israel following the assassination of one of its leaders.

Some of the suicide bombings have been directed at military checkpoints or other military targets inside the occupied territories. Others, including some of those with the most serious civilian casualties, involved attacks on cafés, discos, or other public places in Israeli cities. Those targeting civilians are in violation of international law.

The Palestinian Authority, under both Arafat's and Abbas's leadership, has repeatedly condemned suicide bombings inside Israel. Perhaps more influentially, leading Palestinian intellectuals and activists in the occupied territories and internationally have also rejected suicide attacks on civilians as a legitimate tactic of resistance, identifying them both as morally unacceptable and politically counterproductive.

## Why are only Palestinians carrying out these suicide bombings?

The pattern of bombings reflects the anger and hopelessness that has become endemic among the 3.2 million Palestinians living under military occupation. While organizations certainly orchestrate the attacks, the willingness of young people to contemplate suicide as an acceptable option reflects the widespread personal desperation caused by conditions of occupation. A historical examination of the history of suicide bombings (a history in which the Hindu Tamil Tiger guerrillas of Sri Lanka, not any Islamist organization, hold pride of place) indicates that foreign military occupation is the single most important factor driving such attacks.

People become willing to use their own body as a weapon when other means are unavailable. Because Palestinians have neither an organized army nor the plethora of F-16s, helicopter gunships, tanks, and armored bulldozers that fill Israel's arsenal, the bodies of young men and women become weapons instead.

## What is the Wall that Israel is building in the occupied territories?

Known to Palestinians as the "Apartheid Wall," Israeli officials claim that the huge wall being built in the western sector of the West Bank is designed to protect Israel by keeping potential attackers out. Begun in 2002, and supported by both the Labor Party and the right-wing Likud, the Wall, made of 24-foot-high cement blocks, and including electric fences, trenches,

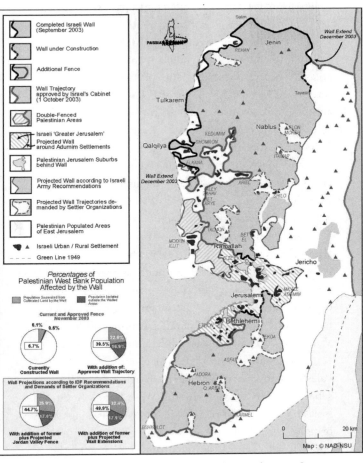

*Permission to reprint graciously provided by the Palestine Liberation Organization*

gun emplacements, and security patrols, is planned eventually to extend to the full length of the West Bank.

But the Wall was not built to follow the Green Line, as the border between Israel and the West Bank is called; instead it curves significantly eastward in many areas to encompass huge swathes of Palestinian land— settlement blocs, large tracts of Palestinian farmland, and major Palestinian water sources—on the Israeli side. According to the UN, in the Jerusalem area alone, 55,000 Palestinians live in the area between the Green Line and the Wall—an area that in some places will become a closed military zone. Thousands of acres of Palestinian land on both sides of the Wall are being seized by the Israeli military and cleared of houses or farmland. Palestinian farmers are supposed to be allowed to cross the Wall to farm their land, but in many areas the Wall extends for huge distances without access gates. Israeli and Palestinian human rights organizations estimate that when completed, and matched by the planned parallel wall in the Jordan Valley, 90,000 Palestinians will have lost their land.

The Wall completely surrounds the large Palestinian town of Qalqilya in the northern West Bank, separating the town from the West Bank. Besides isolating its population, the effect will also include bringing the valuable Western Aquifer System entirely under Israeli control, since its Palestinian portion lies beneath additional lands to be seized in Qalqilya.

In 2003, Israel announced it would build another wall down the Jordan Valley, thus effectively sealing off a truncated, non-contiguous set of West Bank cantons with impenetrable steel. The result will be to ensure Sharon's stated goal of allowing a Palestinian "entity" of no more than about 40 percent of the West Bank, in several non-contiguous chunks, plus most of Gaza.

As the Palestinian human rights group LAW points out, under the Fourth Geneva Convention, to which Israel is a signatory, the destruction or seizure of property in occupied territories is forbidden, as is collective punishment. Article 47 outlines that occupying powers must not make changes to property in occupied territories. Seizure of land in occupied territories is prohibited under Article 52 of the Hague Regulations of 1907, which is a part of customary international law. And according to international humanitarian law governing occupation, occupiers cannot make any changes in the status of occupied territories. Israel's Apartheid Wall seizes land, destroys, and permanently changes the status of occupied territories.

The United Nations estimates that the Wall cuts off at least fifteen percent of West Bank land, and tens of thousands of Palestinians from the West Bank, leaving them on the western, or Israeli, side of the Wall. Significant West Bank aquifers that provide much of the water for Israel's high-tech agricultural production are also located on Palestinian land that will end up in Israeli hands. Within the Wall-enclosed Palestinian areas, hundreds of Israeli military-run checkpoints remain in place, cutting off most towns and especially smaller villages from each other and from the larger cities that once provided commercial, educational, medical, and cultural facilities. Some towns, such as Qalqilya, are now completely cut off, physically surrounded by the Wall and dependent on the whim of Israeli soldiers, who control the only two gates into the town.

By 2005, Israeli officials (including soon-to-be Foreign Minister Tzipi Livni) had admitted that they intended the route of the Wall to be the basis for the future, unilaterally imposed border of an expanded Israeli state.

**What does the rest of the world think about the Wall?**
In December 2003, the UN General Assembly requested that the International Court of Justice in the Hague advise them on the legality of the Wall. In its July 9, 2004, opinion, the ICJ ruled explicitly that the Wall was illegal and that Israel must stop construction and dismantle any part of the Wall inside the occupied territory, including Arab East Jerusalem. "Israel," the ICJ said, "is under an obligation to terminate its breaches of international law; it is under an obligation to cease forthwith the works of construction of the wall being built in the Occupied Palestinian Territory, including in and around East Jerusalem, to dismantle forthwith the structure therein situated, and to repeal or render ineffective forthwith all legislative and regulatory acts relating thereto." Significantly, the ICJ opinion was not limited to the Wall alone. It also stressed the illegality of all the settlements built throughout the Palestinian territory, and in doing so linked the illegality of the Wall

to that of the broader settlement project Israel had undertaken since its occupation of the West Bank, Gaza, and East Jerusalem in the 1967 war.

Israel rejected the ICJ's opinion before it was even issued. In January 2004, Israel's then Prime Minister Ariel Sharon admitted that the Wall was causing problems for ordinary Palestinians, and that the route of the Wall, which cut off huge swathes of West Bank territory, could cause "legal difficulties in defending the state's position." But he went on to assert that "there will be no change as a result of Palestinian or UN demands, including those from the [International] court." Then Justice Minister Yosef Lapid called on his own government to move the Wall, recognizing that "the present route will bring upon us isolation in the world." But Israel continued construction of the Wall on Palestinian land.

The ICJ also stated directly that other countries have their own responsibility to pressure Israel to comply with the court's opinion. "All States," the Court declared, "are under an obligation not to recognize the illegal situation resulting from the construction of the Wall and not to render aid or assistance in maintaining the situation created by such construction." The US government quietly criticized the Wall early in its process of construction, but soon dropped the critique and agreed, in direct violation of the Court's ruling on the obligation of other states, to pay Israel almost $50 million—taken out of the $200 million the US provided in humanitarian support to Palestinian NGOs——to construct check-points and gates in the Wall.

### Why do South African Nobel Peace Prize laureates Nelson Mandela and Archbishop Desmond Tutu, former President Jimmy Carter, and others describe Israel's policies toward the Palestinians as "apartheid"?

The word "apartheid" is the Afrikaans word for "apartness" or "separate." The term came into use in the 1930s, and in 1948 became the official policy of the white South African government, and referred to a system of segregation institutionalized to maintain the supremacy of one group over another. Since that time, the term has most often been used to describe white-dominated governments in South Africa, the former Rhodesia (now Zimbabwe), and the former South-West Africa (now Namibia).

But "apartheid" refers to a system, not only specific to southern Africa. In 1973, the United Nations General Assembly passed the International Convention on the Suppression and Punishment of the Crime of Apartheid. The Convention defined the "crime of apartheid" as a crime against humanity, one that was not specific to South Africa. The crime of apartheid is based on racial segregation and discrimination, and included a list of "inhuman acts" that, if committed to establish and maintain domination of one racial group over any other racial group, would result in systematic oppression and be identified as "apartheid." These acts include murder of the subordinate group's members; denying its members "the right to life and liberty"; inflicting "serious bodily or mental harm, by the infringement of their freedom or dignity, or by subjecting them to torture or to cruel, inhuman or degrading treatment or punishment"; "arbitrary arrest and illegal imprisonment"; imposing on the group's members' "living conditions calculated to cause its or their physical destruction in whole or in part."

The convention goes on to describe "inhuman acts" that could constitute the crime of apartheid actions that bar the subordinate group's participation in the "political, social, economic and cultural life of the country, and the deliberate creation of conditions preventing the full development of such a group or groups, in particular by denying to members... basic human rights and freedoms, including the right to work, the right to form recognized trade unions, the right to education, the right to leave and to return to their country, the right to a nationality, the right to freedom of movement and resident, the right to freedom of opinion and expression, and the right to freedom of peaceful assembly and association." Other such acts include measures "designed to divide the population... by the creation of separate reserves and ghettos for the members of a racial group or groups, the prohibition of mixed marriages... the expropriation of landed property," and finally, measures that deprive people and organizations of their "fundamental rights and freedoms because they oppose apartheid."

Certainly there are significant historical and political differences between the well-known practices of South African apartheid and the system of discrimination against Palestinians that Israel practices. In South Africa the discrimination was based on race, while in Israel the parallel categories are Jew and non-Jew, and there are differences regarding citizenship and other issues. But there are significant parallels as well, both in the histories of South African and Israeli apartheid systems and in the practices themselves. These similarities include laws that divide families, preventing black South Africans or non-Jewish Israelis from owning land, discrimination in education, employment, social services, and more. Further, there is analogous, though clearly not identical, history of earlier pre-state persecution of the dominant group (Afrikaners and Jews), and a comparable form of settler colonialism in both cases, which included the Afrikaner and Zionist settlers themselves turning against their colonial overlords in Britain. One of the most important parallels, though, is the fact that South African apartheid and Israeli apartheid both were and are fundamentally about control of land. The ideologies of racial, national, and religious discrimination were created and imposed to justify the consolidation of power over land and labor. In South Africa, the apartheid government controlled all the land by keeping the non-white labor force under control in urban townships and distant bantustans. In Palestine, the Zionist goal of controlling as much land as possible without Palestinians led to the large-scale expulsions and exiles of 1947–1948 and 1967, and later to the creation of truncated, divided, bantustan-like cantons in the West Bank to allow Israeli control through settlements, a matrix of Jews-only roads and bridges, and annexation of huge swathes of territory.

Some argue that because the term "apartheid" is so fraught with history, so compelling in evoking injustice, that it should not under any circumstances be used against Israel, because Jews were themselves victims of such a great historical injustice in the Holocaust. But criticism of Israel is not the same as criticism of Jews. Israel may define itself as a "Jewish state" or the "state of all the Jews in the world," but Israel is a powerful, modern nation-state, which must, like any other country, be held accountable both for its accomplishments and for its violations of international law. Many Jews, in Israel, in South Africa, in the US, and elsewhere around the world, reject the claim that Israel speaks for them. They believe that precisely because the term "apartheid" so powerfully describes the effect of Israeli policies on Palestinians, it should become the term of choice to describe the systematic Israeli occupation of Palestinian land and denial of Palestinians' equal rights.

### What was the significance of Yasir Arafat's death?
Yasir Arafat, the long-time Palestinian leader who had become synonymous with the struggle and the movement he led, died on November 11, 2004.

Whatever his weaknesses, and they were many, Arafat had played a crucial role in building a national identity and a movement that kept intact and unified the three disparate components of the Palestinian people: those living under Israeli occupation in the West Bank, Gaza and East Jerusalem; those who remained as citizens inside Israel; and those millions of refugees and exiles who languished in impoverished camps or lived scattered across the globe far from their homeland. He had been elected chairman of the Palestine Liberation Organization in 1969, and in 1996 was elected president of the Palestinian Authority, the quasi-governing structure in the West Bank and Gaza created by the 1993 Oslo peace process.

Throughout his political life Arafat proved far more willing to shift and compromise his position than most international observers gave him credit for. After years of holding to the goal of establishing a democratic, secular state in all of Palestine, he led the PLO to its historic 1988 concession of recognizing Israel and accepting as a goal the creation of a Palestinian state limited to the West Bank, Gaza, and East Jerusalem—together comprising only 22 percent of the land of the historic British mandate Palestine. He managed the transition from a liberation movement to a government, despite the challenge posed by the lack of real power or independence for the Palestinian Authority.

And perhaps most importantly, he kept the question of Palestine at the top of the global agenda to a degree unprecedented by any national movement since Vietnam. Arafat went to the United Nations to demand recognition in 1974, and quickly won an observer seat in the global organization for the PLO. And when he declared a putative Palestinian "state" in 1988 in the context of recognizing Israel and accepting a two-state solution, Arafat's action was quickly followed by a diplomatic initiative that led to full diplomatic relations for Palestine with over 110 countries.

His death followed more than two years of an Israeli-orchestrated and US-backed campaign to isolate and marginalize Arafat in an effort to force even greater political concessions from the Palestinians. During Israel's spring 2002 offensive, which included massive assaults by ground troops re-occupying most West Bank cities, Arafat's presidential compound in Ramallah was attacked and largely destroyed by the Israel military. The compound remained besieged for ten days. Although Israeli officials claimed they did not intend to attack Arafat personally, they made clear that if he left the country, he would not be allowed to return. As a result, Arafat spent the next two years in his crumbling compound, leaving only to seek treatment in Paris in the last weeks before his death.

Despite relentless criticism from his own constituents as well as from international leaders, no Palestinian leader ever came close to Arafat's hold on the emotional loyalty of Palestinians of every political stripe. His last two years focused on ultimately failed efforts to maintain political and organizational coherence among the various PLO and Palestinian Authority security and political agencies, with Arafat's longstanding goal of leading a truly independent and viable Palestinian state giving way to the reality of presiding over an Authority reduced to squabbling over crumbs of derivative power.

Many world leaders, particularly those in countries that had faced their own struggles for independence from colonial control, issued powerful statements of respect and shared grief at the news of Arafat's passing. But for Israel, the US, and other powerful countries, pro forma expressions of condolence quickly gave way to barely con-cealed statements of happiness that Arafat was gone from the scene. Only now, Western leaders claimed, could what was quickly anointed the "post-Arafat era" result in a chance for an Israeli–Palestinian peace—based on the assumption that any "post-Arafat" leader would be even more compliant to US–Israeli demands.

### What does the Israeli–Palestinian conflict have to do with the US war in Iraq?

In the run-up to the 2003 US invasion of Iraq, the Bush administration had failed to win international backing or international legitimacy for the war in the UN Security Council; there was widespread global recognition that the war would be illegal. But the US had not given up hope that other governments—particularly that of Britain's Tony Blair—would join its so-called coalition. Britain and others, including Spain, were prepared to endorse Bush's war despite broad public opposition in virtually every country, but they wanted a political trade-off too. For this reason the Bush–Blair announcement of the text of a new "road map" was timed and orchestrated for maximum global visibility, highlighting the links between Iraq and Israel–Palestine just days before the Iraq war was launched.

The "road map" was to be implemented by the so-called Quartet, a diplomatic fiction designed to provide political cover to the Bush administration's unilateral plans for the Middle East by including the European Union, Russia, and the United Nations as part of a team. In fact, the US continued to call the shots, the other three players remained subservient to its plans, and Middle East diplomacy remained stalled. It was particularly unfortunate that the United Nations was coerced into providing political cover to the US through participation in the Quartet a move that seriously discredited the global organization.

In March 2003, the US, backed by the British, invaded and occupied Iraq; less than two months later the UN Security Council recognized the US and UK as "occupying powers" in Iraq, with all the accompanying obligations under international law.

Under the Fourth Geneva Convention, the Palestinians of the West Bank, Gaza, East Jerusalem, and the people of Iraq all constitute "protected" populations, living under foreign occupations. Throughout its years of occupation since 1967, Israel has engaged in practices that constitute serious violations of international law, including torture, extra-judicial assassinations, extended curfews and closures, house demolitions, the destruction of agricultural land and civilian property, expulsions, illegal imprisonment, and other forms of collective punishment. Even before the US invaded Iraq, the Pentagon and other US government agencies were looking to the Israeli occupation as a model for a future US occupation of Iraq—long before the Bush administration even admitted its plan to invade Iraq. Increasingly, the two occupations have come to resemble each other, as the occupiers have actively collaborated to consolidate their control over angry populations.

In April 2002, more than a year before the US invaded Iraq, Israel sent troops to fully re-occupy the West Bank. The Israeli military's attack on the Palestinian refugee camp in Jenin led to the killing of dozens of Palestinian civilians, including seven women and nine children. According to Human Rights Watch, "Israeli forces committed serious violations of international humanitarian law, some amounting prima facie to war crimes." But the US viewed the Jenin attack as a model for its planned invasion of Iraq, and US military officials met with the Israeli military to learn the urban warfare techniques that Israel had used in Jenin. Two years later, in April 2004, the US used those same tactics in the attack on Fallujah in Iraq, including the widespread killing of women and children. In a reversed version of collaboration, Israel admitted using white phosphorous munitions during its 2006 war in

Lebanon; the US military has long been condemned for its continued use of this weapon since the Vietnam War.

Further, the torture scandals involving US prisons at Abu Ghraib in Iraq, Guantanamo Bay, and elsewhere reflected many of the same techniques Israel had long used against Palestinian prisoners. The Israeli High Court banned torture in 1999, but the Israeli Public Committee Against Torture indicates that 58 percent of Palestinians detainees report they have been subjected to the same techniques the US troops have used against prisoners in the "global war on terror": beatings, being forced to remain in painful positions, being hooded for long periods, sleep and toilet deprivation, sexual humiliation, and more. The US general in charge of Abu Ghraib in the first months of the US occupation of Iraq told the BBC that Israeli agents were assisting US interrogators throughout the US-run prison system in Iraq.

The US military certainly did not need Israeli help to occupy another country. But Israel's years of occupation allowed it to provide the Pentagon with advice and training in tactics designed to take advantage of specific cultural, religious, and national Arab traditions. The US claims that its occupation of Iraq was "democratizing" the entire Middle East was countered by what people on the ground throughout the region actually saw: the expansion of occupations. Instead of new democracy, the US war and occupation in Iraq were viewed throughout the region as a parallel occupation to the US-backed Israeli occupation of Palestine.

By the time of the 2006 Israeli war against Hezbollah and Lebanon, an even clearer connection had emerged. The Israeli goals of attempting to wipe out all resistance to its control and domination of the region matched almost word-for-word the global US goals being fought out in Iraq. In fact, the strategies had similar origins. In the early 1990s, a group of neoconservative American analysts and former policymakers collaborated on a strategic vision for US foreign policy, which became known as the Project for the New American Century, or PNAC. After September 11, many of their ideas gained dominance, being included in the 2002 National Security Strategy document of President George W. Bush, which set the terms for the invasion and occupation of Iraq. But before that, back in 1996, several of the PNAC authors had traveled to Israel at the request of Benjamin Netanyahu, a conservative and US-oriented Israeli politician then running for prime minister. Their strategy paper, called "Making a Clean Break: Defending the Realm," proposed an almost identical recipe for Israeli foreign policy: focus on military power rather than diplomacy, let all of Israel's neighbors know that force rather than negotiations would be the new basis for relationships, and make a "clean break" with all earlier peace processes, most notably the Oslo process, then in its third year. When Israel went to war against Lebanon in 2006, many saw the "clean break" strategy coming to bloody life.

***What is "transfer"? Why did talk of "transfer" of Palestinians increase during the build-up to war in Iraq?***
Beginning in the spring of 2002, as war fever began to heat up in Washington, the threat of "transfer" became a much more serious concern for Palestinians. Long deemed unacceptable even for polite discussion in Israel, "transfer," Israel's prim euphemism for ethnic cleansing, moved into the forefront of political discussion. Featured prominently in the Israeli media, the subject of at least one high-profile academic conference at one of Israel's most prestigious universities, "transfer" moved into the mainstream of political discussion. Tsomet, the political party that officially calls for "transfer," long part of the Israeli Knesset, was given the Ministry of Tourism portfolio in General Sharon's government.

The specific threat was that in the regional chaos resulting from the US war in Iraq and its aftermath, Israel might forcibly expel some numbers of Palestinians. But the threat remained even after the initial military attacks on Iraq had given way to US occupation of the country. Perhaps it would be in the form of a punishment against a whole village from which a suicide bomber came. Perhaps 500 or 1,000 or so targeted Palestinian individuals—political leaders, intellectuals, militants, or those Israel claims are militants—would be bused over the river into Jordan or flown over Israel's border into Lebanon. Besides the massive expulsions that forced more than one million Palestinians into exile during the 1948 and 1967 wars, Israel had relied on "transfer" as recently as 1994. At that time, Israeli troops arrested 415 Islamists from the occupied Palestinian territories, forced them into military helicopters and flew them into the hills of south Lebanon. There, without documents, without permission, and despite rejection by the Lebanese government, they were abandoned on the snow-covered hillsides.

General Sharon himself, elected prime minister of Israel in January 2001, had initially created the "Jordan is Palestine" campaign in 1981–82 that called for expelling all Palestinians out of the occupied territories and pushing them into Jordan. In 1989, former Israeli Prime Minister Benjamin Netanyahu told students at Bar-Ilan University: "Israel should have exploited the repression of the demonstrations in China, when world attention was focused on that country, to carry out mass expulsions among the Arabs of the territories." Recent mobilizations of Israeli academics have issued public calls against "transfer," but the danger remains very real— 2002 polls showed that more than 40 percent of Israelis are in favor of such ethnic cleansing. Advocates of "transfer" had long participated in Israel's political life. In 2001, Tsomet, a party that officially calls for "transfer," was given the Ministry of Tourism portfolio in Sharon's new government. In 2001, and again in 2003, Avigdor Lieberman, the leader of the Yisrael Beitenu party, made up largely of Russian immigrants, who calls openly for forced transfer of Palestinians, was appointed to other cabinet positions. And in 2006, the ostensibly "moderate" government of Ehud Olmert appointed Lieberman as "Minister of Strategic Threats," with unparalleled authority over dealings with Iran.

### What was Israel's "convergence plan" for the West Bank, and why did President Bush endorse Israel's unilateral 2004 plans to annex much of the West Bank?

In April 2004, US President George W. Bush accepted Israeli Prime Minister Ariel Sharon's unilateral plan to annex the major West Bank settlement blocs and repudiate the internationally recognized Palestinian right of return. The agreement, formalized in an exchange of letters, was a quid pro quo for Israel's decision to unilaterally withdraw the illegal Israeli settlers and redeploy the Israeli troops from the Gaza Strip.

In rejecting the Palestinian right of return and accepting the permanence of Israeli occupation of Palestinian land, Bush essentially banished the possibility of achieving a serious and comprehensive solution to the Palestinian–Israeli conflict. The "new status quo" of US-recognized permanent Israeli occupation, no right of return, and no viable Palestinian state, set the terms for the next indefinite period.

The US position accepting Israel's unilateral decision-making also returned Middle East diplomacy officially to its pre-1991 position, excluding Palestinians from all negotiations. Israeli–US negotiations become the substitute for Israeli–Palestinian talks, with the US free to concede Palestinian land and rights. As one PLO legal advisor told the *New York Times*, "imagine if Palestinians said, 'O.K., we give California to Canada.' Americans should stop wondering why they have so little credibility in the Middle East."

The US endorsement reaffirmed the US willingness to violate international law, ignore the United Nations Charter, and undermine UN resolutions (including the often-cited Resolution 242, which unequivocally prohibits "the acquisition of territory by force") to provide diplomatic and political protection for Israel. It even violated the terms of the US-imposed but internationally endorsed "road map," the first phase of which stipulated that Israel must freeze all settlement activity. Sharon stated explicitly that the six major settlement blocs should continue to grow and be strengthened.

Government officials and commentators from around the world have been unified in condemning Bush's statements. UN Secretary General Kofi Annan criticized the US endorsement of Israel's unilateral plan, stating that "final status issues should be determined in negotiations between the parties based on relevant Security Council resolutions."

Sharon's "Gaza disengagement" plan was part of a strategy to end Israeli–Palestinian negotiations. Sharon made clear that he viewed the pull-back of troops and settlers as part of a "long-term interim solution," in which Israeli occupation would be retooled to remain in place virtually forever, without ever reaching "final status" negotiations. That meant giving up the Gaza settlements, and shifting the military control of Gaza, at least until the re-occupation that occurred in July 2006, from inside its cities and towns to positions surrounding and controlling it from outside.

The Gaza settlements, while economically valuable for Israel (not surprising given that the 8,000 settlers controlled 40 percent of the land and 40 percent of the water of the 1.4 million Palestinian residents of the Gaza Strip) were still costly, because the small number of settlers depended on significant numbers of Israeli troops for protection. So giving up the Gaza settlements was a small price to pay for consolidating Israeli control over the much more valuable land of the West Bank, and guaranteeing permanent US support for Israeli annexation of the huge West Bank settlement blocs and even more land encompassed within the Apartheid Wall.

This strategy of giving up Gaza settlements to annex West Bank land became known as the "convergence plan" when Ehud Olmert took over as prime minister in March 2006, after the incurable stroke that three months earlier ended the political career of Ariel Sharon. Following Israel's serious defeat in the Lebanon war that summer, Olmert's Sharon-linked popularity quickly declined, and his plan to evacuate some tens of thousands of West Bank settlers, while leaving 80 percent of the 240,000 settlers in place, evaporated. Israelis no longer seemed willing to envision even a small-scale symbolic withdrawal to provide political cover to the much larger-scale annexation of prime Palestinian land. Instead, a potentially indefinite continuation of the unstable status quo loomed.

### What is Hamas?

Hamas is a Palestinian Islamist and nationalist organization. It believes in a form of political Islam in which religion forms the basis for social and political strategy. Its origins are in the Muslim Brotherhood, a pan-Arab Islamist organization based in Egypt. Hamas was created in Gaza in December 1987, immediately following the eruption of the first Palestinian intifada. In the first years of its existence, Israel allowed Hamas to gain popularity without any of the repression and obstacles it imposed on the secular PLO. In fact, Israeli strategists viewed Hamas as a potential competitor with the PLO for Palestinian loyalty, and believed the Islamist organization would be less of a serious challenge to Israel than the nationalist PLO. Although the PLO is itself a coalition of organizations, Hamas was never a member of the PLO.

Throughout its years, Hamas's activities have always been far broader than those of its well-known military wing. Especially in Gaza, always the poorest part of Palestine, Hamas created a widespread network of social welfare agencies, including schools, clinics, hospitals, mosques, and more. During the years of the first intifada (1987–1993), as well as the years of the Oslo process and the Palestinian Authority (from 1993 on), Hamas provided many of the basic services that Israel as the occupying power refused to provide, and that the PA, lacking real power and facing both poverty and problems of corruption, could not. As a result, Hamas's popularity grew.

Hamas's first suicide bombing was in 1993, and for many in Israel and internationally, that method of attack came to characterize the organization. Some of the attacks were against Israeli soldiers in the occupied territories—acts of military resistance authorized under international law—but others targeted civilians inside Israel itself, in violation of international law. Hamas declared a unilateral ceasefire in March 2005, which it maintained until June 2006, when it announced its intention to break the ceasefire in response to a continuing and then escalating set of Israeli attacks. Of particular relevance in the Hamas decision was the Israeli attack just days before on a Gaza beach that killed nine Palestinians, seven of them from one family, including five children. The end of the ceasefire led to Hamas's attack on an Israeli military patrol just over the Gaza border, culminating in the capture of one Israeli soldier.

Israel has targeted many Hamas leaders for assassination, including Sheikh Ahmed Yassin, the paralyzed and wheelchair-bound founder and spiritual leader of Hamas, who was killed by an Israeli missile in Gaza in March 2004. His position was taken over by Abdel Aziz Rantisi, who was killed by Israel a month later. Rantisi, a Gaza physician, was among the 400 Hamas activists kidnapped by Israel and expelled to Lebanon in the early 1990s. Returned to Gaza in a prisoner exchange, Rantisi was assassinated by a "targeted" Israeli missile strike in Gaza. In another ostensibly "targeted" assassination, this time of Hamas leader Salah Shihadeh, fourteen other people, nine of them children, were killed by the Israeli military air strike. State Department officials reportedly attempted to warn then Secretary of State Colin Powell about Israel possibly violating the US Arms Export Control Act through its use of US-provided weapons in the assassination. But according to *US News and World Report*, then Undersecretary of State and later US Ambassador to the United Nations John Bolton prevented the warning from being passed on to Powell.

International observers, including US govern-ment officials and mainstream media, often misrepresented Hamas's political stance, which changed in response to political developments over the years. For years, Hamas had rejected a two-state solution, holding out for what it called an Islamic state in all of historic Palestine. But the Palestinian majority that elected Hamas in January 2006 included many who did not endorse that program. And in the midst of the summer 2006 Israeli attacks on Gaza, Hamas leader and Palestinian Prime Minister Ismail Haniyeh wrote in the *Washington Post* that the Gaza crisis was part of a "wider national conflict that can be resolved only by addressing the full dimensions of Palestinian national rights in an integrated manner. This means statehood for the West Bank and Gaza, a capital in Arab East Jerusalem, and resolving the 1948 Palestinian refugee issue fairly, on the basis of international legitimacy and established law." That carefully articulated set of Palestinian goals—clearly "moderate" even by US and European standards—matched closely what Haniyeh called Palestinian "priorities." Those included "recognition of the core dispute over the land of historical Palestine and the rights of all its people; resolution of the refugee issue from 1948; reclaiming all lands occupied in 1967; and stopping Israeli attacks, assassinations and military expansion." It was significant that the Hamas leader, often accused of calling for "the destruction of Israel," actually distinguished between the need to "recognize" all the lost lands and rights of pre-1948 historical Palestine and the need for Palestinians to "reclaim" only those lands occupied in 1967.

### Why did the Palestinians choose Hamas in the January 2006 elections?

The January 2006 Palestinian elections were an imperfect exercise in democracy, since they were inevitably held under conditions of military occupation. However, it is clear that the results represented a reasonably accurate assessment of public opinion. International observers, including former US President Jimmy Carter, representing the US-based Carter Center, called the election "peaceful, competitive, and genuinely democratic."

There are strong indications that huge turn-out for Hamas was not really a statement of support for an Islamist social agenda or for their prior military attacks (Hamas had initiated and maintained its own unilateral ceasefire from early 2005). Rather, it was a call for change in the Palestinians' untenable situation, rejecting the status quo. In his report immediately after the election, Carter recognized that "Fatah, the party of Arafat and Abbas, has become vulnerable because of its political ineffectiveness and alleged corruption." At the time, many Palestinians said that they could have accepted the existing leadership even with its corruption, if only Fatah had any success in ending the occupation, and could have accepted its political failures if only it were not so corrupt. But the combination of corruption and failure was simply too much, and Hamas reaped the electoral results.

Israeli leaders immediately responded with claims that they now had "no partner for peace," stated that they would not negotiate with a Hamas-led Palestinian Authority, and called for an international boycott of the new government. But those claims were a red herring—Israel had not been negotiating with the existing (Fatah-led, non-Hamas) Palestinian Authority for more than two years, having chosen instead a strategy of unilateral action to redraw borders and impose an Israeli "solution" to the conflict.

The US, having already accepted the unilateral, no-negotiations approach of then Prime Minister Ariel Sharon, including Israel's abandonment of the US-backed "road map," also promoted the Israeli call for an international boycott and sanctions against the Palestinians. And it was US pressure on Europe, Arab states, and many other US allies to accept the boycott that was largely responsible for the humanitarian crisis that soon hit the occupied territories, especially Gaza. For example, when some Arab banks announced plans to transmit humanitarian assistance donated to beleaguered Palestinians, the US announced that the US branches of those banks would face serious sanctions. Not surprisingly, the banks withdrew their plans, and the Palestinians did not get the funds.

The result was a dramatic rise in the already dangerous humanitarian crisis. In a rare joint statement in July 2006, UN agencies stated that they were "alarmed by developments on the ground, which have seen innocent civilians, including children, killed, brought increased misery to hundreds of thousands of people, and which will wreak far-reaching harm on Palestinian society. An already alarming situation in Gaza, with poverty rates at nearly eighty percent and unemployment at nearly forty percent, is likely to deteriorate rapidly, unless immediate and urgent action is taken." The UN's overall coordinating body, OCHA (Office for Coordinating Humanitarian Assistance), called on Israel to allow UN deliveries of emergency supplies, but recognized that "humanitarian assistance is not enough to prevent suffering. With the [Israeli] bombing of the [Gaza] electric plant, the lives of 1.4 million people, almost half of them children, worsened overnight. The Government of Israel should repair the damage done to the power station. Obligations under international humanitarian law, applying to both parties, include preventing harm to civilians and destroying civilian infrastructure and also refraining from collective measures, intimidation and reprisals. Civilians are disproportionately paying the price of this conflict."

### What are Israel's "targeted assassinations"?

"Targeted assassination" is Israel's euphemism for its deliberate killing of Palestinian militants or leaders. In legal language, this is known as "extra-judicial killing," referring to a government's decision to kill someone without charges, without trial, and without any kind of judicial proceeding. Israel has carried out such killings of Palestinians since the 1970s, but the use of so-called targeted assassinations became far more commonplace with the beginning of the second intifada in 2000.

The term "targeted assassination" is designed to disguise two huge problems. First, the "targeting" is not so precise. According to the Israeli human rights organization B'Tselem, of 331 Palestinians killed in "targeted assassination" operations between September 2000 and June 2006, 127 were not targets at all; many of them were women and children. Second, calling these killings "targeted" does not make them legal; the Fourth Geneva Convention prohibits *all* killings by the occupying power of anyone in the occupied population. There are no exceptions.

Most of the assassinations are carried out long-distance—using missiles, rockets, or bombs that hit cars or houses or whole residential neighborhoods. In 2002, the killing of Hamas leader Sheikh Salah Shihadeh at 3AM in a crowded Gaza apartment building resulted in not only his death but also the deaths of fourteen others, including nine children. Four years later, Israel's implementation of the assassination policy escalated again, following the Hamas victory in the Palestinian elections. In response, the Public Committee Against Torture in Israel noted that the problem of people being killed who were not the "official" target was made "abundantly clear during the 7 February 2006 air strike [in Gaza] that killed the two targeted people but also injured four children, one critically." A few months after that attack, on July 12, another Israeli air assault on a Gaza house, missed the "targeted" Hamas leader, but did kill two other adults and seven children.

The Fourth Geneva Convention, under Article 3 (1) (a) prohibits all "violence to life and person" and "murder of all kinds." Giving murder the clinical term "targeted assassination" does not make it legal. Israel has attempted to disguise the clear illegality of these killings by asserting that each is individually approved by the Prime Minister; but in fact, the authorization by any Israeli official, or even by Israel's highest courts, is thoroughly irrelevant as a defense to the Geneva Convention's absolute prohibition.

### Didn't Israel's occupation of Gaza end with its withdrawal of soldiers and settlers in 2005?

Israel's then Prime Minister Ariel Sharon announced in 2002 his intention to unilaterally "disengage" from the Gaza Strip, removing the 8,000 or so Israeli settlers and all soldiers from the territory. As the occupying power, Israel certainly had the unilateral obligation to end its occupation, remove its soldiers and its illegal settlements (all the Gaza settlements, as well as all those in the West Bank and in occupied East Jerusalem, are illegal, built in violation of the Geneva Conventions), and stop illegal acts, such as the demolition of over 3,000 Palestinian houses since 2000. But Sharon's action in Gaza was not designed to lead to an end to all of Israel's occupation. Rather, it was part of a strategically calculated plan to end Israeli–Palestinian negotiations, and to impose instead what Sharon once called a "long-term interim solution" in which the Israeli occupation would be retooled to remain in place without ever reaching "final status" negotiations. Further, it would get rid of Israel's costly occupation of the impoverished and thirsty Gaza Strip, while gaining crucial US support for permanent annexation of huge swathes of territory in the far wealthier, more strategic, and water-rich West Bank.

The carefully planned removal of Gaza settlers in the summer of 2005 showed a powerful picture of grieving families being forcibly—if gently—removed from their homes. Israel offered each settler family hundreds of thousands of dollars in compensation, and new homes were quickly made available in Israeli towns or, ironically, in equally illegal West Bank settlements. Groups of settler families wishing to remain together were assured of neighboring homes wherever they wished to move. It was a humane response to the inevitably sad human cost of forcible relocation (although all the settlers knew they were living on occupied territory in violation of international law). And it was a far cry from the fifteen-minute get-out-with-whatever-you-can-carry warnings in most, and the complete lack of compensation in all, of Israel's expulsions and house demolitions of Palestinians throughout the West Bank, East Jerusalem, and Gaza Strip.

Following the Israeli redeployment, Gaza's territory was free of Israeli soldiers and settlers, but remained surrounded and under complete Israeli control: Israel continued to control Gaza's economy, withholding $50 million or so of Palestinian monthly tax revenues, prohibiting Palestinian workers from entering Israel, and controlling the Israeli and Egyptian border crossings into and out of Gaza for all goods and people. Israel forcibly limited the range of Gaza's fleet of fishermen. It controlled Gaza's airspace and coastal waters, and continued to prohibit construction of a seaport or rebuilding the airport. And after the election of the Hamas-led government in January 2006, Israel continued its air strikes and ground attacks on people and infrastructure throughout Gaza, and its almost nightly barrage of sonic sound-bombs across Gaza's population centers. Under international law, such a siege constitutes a continuation of occupation.

Conditions in Gaza rapidly deteriorated; by early 2006 UN and other humanitarian agencies were reporting widespread hunger; unemployment spiked over 60 percent in many areas, and long-term Israeli closures of the border crossings meant virtually no Gazan produce could reach the market. The rate of absolute poverty—of people living on less than $2 per day—rose to 78 percent, an unprecedented level.

In June 2006, Israel responded to a border skirmish in which an Israeli soldier was captured, with a full-scale armed assault on Gaza, including air, sea, and ground attacks. Israeli commandos carried out midnight raids in Gaza (as well as many West Bank cities) to kidnap Hamas legislators and Cabinet ministers of the Palestinian Authority. The *New York Times* quoted Prime Minister Ehud Olmert saying that despite the earlier claims of "disengagement," Israel would continue to act militarily in Gaza as it wished, "We will operate, enter, and pull out as needed."

### Why did Hamas capture an Israeli soldier in June 2006 after Israel had withdrawn its troops and settlers from Gaza in 2005?

The occupation of Gaza did not end with the withdrawal of settlers and soldiers. After the pull-out, Gaza remained besieged and surrounded, and Israel remained in complete control of all aspects of Gazan economic, political, and social life. According to international law, occupation is defined as the complete control of a territory and its people—so the withdrawal of troops and settlers meant changing the form of occupation, not the essence.

In January 2006 the Palestinian Authority held elections. The Islamist organization Hamas won a majority of votes (see page 65). In response to the election of Hamas, internationally recognized as fair, the US backed Israel's call for an international boycott and sanctions against the elected government, cutting all financial aid, punishing banks that might allow transfer of funds, and isolating the Palestinian Authority. Throughout the spring of 2006, conditions deteriorated across the occupied territories, with impoverished Gaza the worst hit. Unemployment in Gaza hovered near 70 percent, and poverty rates climbed to almost 80 percent. UN officials feared a humanitarian crisis. Israel continued its arrests and "targeted assassinations," and in June a family of seven, including five children, was killed by Israel's shelling of a Gaza beach. In response to the escalating Israeli attacks, the ongoing economic boycott, and the skyrocketing humanitarian crisis, Hamas called off its then–sixteen-month-long unilateral ceasefire. The capture of the Israeli soldier followed two weeks later. In early July 2006, the Israeli newspaper *Ha'aretz* reported that Israel's attorney general had acknowledged that the plan to send troops back into Gaza had been decided weeks earlier. (Also in July, while the Israeli assault on Lebanon was underway, both *Ha'aretz* and the *San Francisco Chronicle* reported that the Israeli military's war plan for Lebanon had been in the works for two to four years, with officials waiting for the opportune moment to launch the attack.)

*Doesn't Israel have the right to defend itself against Hamas in Gaza, as well as against Hezbollah in Lebanon?*
Every country has the right to defend itself and its citizens, against attack. But no country has the right to violate international law against others in the name of its own self-defense. Israel claims its right of self-defense includes the "right" to attack much of Gaza's infrastructure—starting with Gaza's only power-generating plant—and to kill scores of Gaza civilians, because Hamas captured an Israeli soldier. But according to international law, there is no justification for Israel's assault in Gaza.

The war that Israel launched against Gaza in June 2006 and against Lebanon weeks later began when Israel chose to escalate border skirmishes to full-scale wars against civilian populations. Hamas attacked a military post just over the Gaza border—an act of resistance to occupation considered legal under international law since it was against a military, not civilian target. Similarly, Hezbollah's July 12 raid across the Israeli border may have violated the 1949 armistice agreement between the newly created state of Israel and Lebanon (there was never a peace treaty between them), but the raid was limited to a military target.

As Human Rights Watch described it, "the targeting and capture of enemy soldiers is allowed under international humanitarian law." In both cases Israel responded first with cross-border raids of their own to try to get its captured soldiers back, legal under international law. But, it was Israel that then took the step of escalating from a small-scale border skirmish into full-scale war—by immediately launching major attacks against civilian targets. Israel destroyed the only power plant in Gaza, plunging 800,000 Gaza residents into months of hot, thirsty darkness at the height of the desert summer. In Lebanon, Israel began by attacking key bridges linking towns in southern Lebanon and destroying the international airport, before escalating further to full-scale assaults on the total infrastructure and civilian population of southern Lebanon, and much of Beirut and the rest of the country.

It must be stated unequivocally that this was a war against civilians—there was nothing "collateral" about the violence. Israel was responsible for this war. During the initial clashes on Israel's borders with both Gaza and Lebanon, the only Israelis killed or captured were soldiers; no civilians were targeted or harmed until Israel chose to transform those military border skirmishes into wars aimed directly at Gaza's and Lebanon's civilian populations. Hezbollah violated international law as well, with its indiscriminate rocket attacks against targets in Israeli cities, but it did not begin those attacks until 36 hours after Israel's assault against civilians began, and only after announcing publicly its desire to negotiate prisoner exchange. Given the human devastation of the predictable Israeli response, Hezbollah's initial raid may have been what French Foreign Minister Philippe Douste-Blazy called an "irresponsible act," but that was far different from Israel's brutal response, which was, he said, "a disproportionate act of war." The Israeli attacks stood in stark violation of numerous Geneva Convention prohibitions: against collective punishment, against targeting civilians, against destruction of civilian infrastructure, and more. The attacks constituted war crimes.

Explanations in the media and elsewhere disagree about which party is responsible for the conflict because analysts choose to begin their chronologies at different points. In the US media, most mainstream outlets and commentators claimed the summer 2006 war began when Hamas captured an Israeli soldier. But that act cannot be arbitrarily separated from the immediate spark of Israel's attack on a Gaza beach a week earlier, which led to Hamas calling off its sixteen-month-long unilateral ceasefire. It could not be separated from the reality of a decades-old illegal Israeli occupation of Gaza that began in 1967—let alone from the economic isolation, closures, and military attacks that had escalated through that spring. As Gideon Levy wrote in the Israeli newspaper *Ha'aretz*, Israelis and most Americans always start with the assumption that the Palestinians started it. "'They started' will be the routine response to anyone who tries to argue, for example, that a few hours before the first Qassam [rocket] fell on the school in Ashkelon [a city inside Israel], causing no damage, Israel sowed destruction at the Islamic University in Gaza. Israel is causing electricity blackouts, laying sieges, bombing and shelling, assassinating and imprisoning, killing and wounding civilians, including children and babies, in horrifying numbers, but 'they started' ."

And the crisis built on the existing humanitarian crisis underway in Gaza, a result of US and Israeli-orchestrated international sanctions against the Palestinians that began with the January election of the Hamas-led parliament. That collective punish-ment represented a clear violation of the Fourth Geneva Convention, which deals with the protection of occupied populations. Article 33 states, "No protected person may be punished for an offense he or she has not personally committed. Collective penalties and likewise all measures of intimidation or of terrorism are prohibited." In Article 36 the "taking of hostages is prohibited." That meant the Israeli arrests of about one-third of the elected Palestinian Legislative Assembly and about one-half of the Palestinian Authority's cabinet ministers, whom Israel kidnapped largely to serve as bargaining chips, were illegal.

# PART II

# THE OTHER PLAYERS: THE ROLE OF THE US, THE UN, ARAB STATES, AND EUROPE

*Why is the Israeli–Palestinian conflict so important on the global stage? Why does the rest of the world care, and get so involved, in this conflict in such a small place?*

Global interest in Israel–Palestine reflects two different kinds of concerns: personal (including religious affiliation and national or ethnic bonds) and strategic (including military, diplomatic, economic, and other considerations). As the site of holy places of all three of the world's main monotheistic religions, it is perhaps inevitable that passions will run high.

In its earliest days Palestine was a crossroads of trade between three continents. Since 1967 Israel played an important role as a Cold War ally and sometimes military surrogate of the US. Today Israel stands as one of perhaps the two or three closest US allies, and for most nations around the world, maintaining good relations with Washington requires at least amicable ties to Israel.

Today Palestine stands at the symbolic center of much of Arab and Muslim consciousness, giving it a regional and indeed international significance far beyond its size. Palestine is also, since the independence of East Timor in 1999, one of the last remnants of a once far more common phenomenon: what the UN used to call "non–self-governing territories." In other words, colonies occupied by another nation.

## *What is the international response to the Israeli– Palestinian conflict? Is there international agreement?*

Since at least the mid-1970s, when the Palestine Liberation Organization was deemed the sole legitimate representative of the Palestinian people and welcomed as an observer member of the United Nations, there has been a clear international consensus on how to deal with the seemingly endless conflict.

Security Council Resolution 242, passed after the 1967 war, is widely recognized as the basis for a permanent settlement. Outside of the US, however, the resolution is understood in a much different way than simply calling for an exchange of land for peace. The international consensus puts much greater emphasis than the US does on the opening of the resolution, which unequivocally asserts "the inadmissibility of the acquisition of territory by war." That is understood to mean that the territory Israel captured by war must be returned; that to keep it is "inadmissible."

In terms of process, the international community has long recognized as inadequate the notion of bilateral talks under US sponsorship, in which Israel and Palestine, with such enormous disparities of power, face each other as if on a level playing field. That they are forced to negotiate before a mediator that is itself the strategic, financial, diplomatic, and military champion of the stronger of the two parties only makes matters less legitimate. Instead, the UN has repeatedly called for convening an international peace conference, in which all the parties to the conflict, including Israel, the PLO, the Arab states, and others would negotiate in concert under the auspices of the UN Security Council.

### Why hasn't the US been part of that consensus?

The US has, since 1967, strongly opposed inter-nationalizing the conflict. The US maintained the view that multilateral talks would amount to other countries unfairly ganging up on Israel, and that the US itself was the only outside power with a legitimate right to lead, or even participate in, negotiations. As a result, even diplomatic efforts with a patina of international legitimacy, such as the Madrid peace talks in 1991, were fundamentally reduced to separate and unequal bilateral talks between Israel and each Arab party. (The Israeli—Palestinian talks in Madrid, in fact, did not even constitute an independent track, but rather were orchestrated as a sub-set of the Israeli—Jordanian talks.)

### Why is the US the central player in the Middle East?

The main reason is power. By the time Israel was created, with the end of the British Mandate over Palestine, World War II was just over and the European powers, victors and losers alike, lay decimated by war. Of all the major powers, only the US survived the war intact, with economic and military power on the rise, and hungry for oil.

The US spent the Cold War years locked in contention with the Soviet Union, as much as anywhere else vying for influence in the strategic Middle East. With the end of the Cold War, the collapse of the Soviet Union, and the US victory in the 1991 Gulf War, which profoundly altered the Middle East in favor of even greater US influence, Washington's super-power status has only expanded. Today, the US, despite a rising challenge from Iran, remains the controlling authority in shaping the political map of the region.

The combination of the US–Israeli "special relationship" and the vast superiority of Israel's power in the region further consolidates the US centrality. As long as Israel remains the strongest military force in the region, with the fifth most powerful nuclear arsenal in the world and one of the most powerful conventional militaries anywhere, other countries in the region and around the world have tended to limit their diplomatic imagination to what they think Israel will accept. So far, that has meant acquiescence to continued US control.

### What explains the US–Israeli "special relationship"?

When Israel was first created, its leaders chose to maintain the clearly Euro-American, rather than Middle Eastern, orientation that had characterized the Zionist movement even before the state was founded. With statehood, Israel maintained its military reliance on France, Czechoslovakia, and other European powers, but it would soon turn for help and support to the leading Western power, the post–World War II United States.

Even before the State of Israel was declared, US support was strong, but it remained diplomatically and financially "normal" until the time of the 1967 War. When Israel demonstrated the extraordinary military prowess that destroyed three Arab armies and occupied parts of four countries, the US quickly recognized Israel's potential as a valuable Cold War ally, and the friendly alliance segued into the all-embracing "special relationship" and the strategic alliance that continues today. Economic assistance, military aid, and diplomatic protection all soared. Within US society, support for Israel grew exponentially as existing pro-Israeli organizations (mostly but not entirely based in the US Jewish community) dramatically increased their influence in popular culture, in education, in the media, and among policymakers. Members of Congress who criticized Israeli violations or voted evenhandedly on legislation concerning the Middle East have been regularly punished by the increasingly powerful pro-Israel lobby. Congressman Paul Findley and Senator Charles Percy lost their seats during the 1980s, while Southern African-American Representatives Cynthia McKinney and Earl Hilliard lost in the 2002 primaries after lobby-funded campaigns were launched on behalf of their challengers.

The power of the pro-Israeli lobby grew exponentially from the 1990s on, as right-wing Christian fundamentalist organizations supporting what came to be known as "Christian Zionism" grew in numbers, financing, and political clout. While the traditional, largely Jewish lobby groups such as the American-Israel Political Affairs Committee (AIPAC) and the Council of Presidents of Major Jewish Organizations remained powerful in the Democratic Party and especially influential in Congress, where coordinated fundraising campaigns increased their power, the newer Christian Zionist groups gained strength in the Republican Party, and from 2001 became increasingly prominent in the White House of George W. Bush.

### Is the US an "honest broker" in the conflict?

The US calls itself an honest broker, but that is correct only in a very particular context. The parallel is not that of a baseball umpire, independent and impartial, but rather that of a real estate broker who deals with both parties—honestly or not—but who is known to represent the interests of only one side because her own economic (or in this case strategic) interests depend on it.

Perhaps more dangerously, the US position always refused to place international law and UN resolutions at its center. If it did, the necessity of a complete end to Israel's occupation would be understood as the starting point of any kind of future peace for Israel as well as for the Palestinians.

### How does the US support Israel?

US support for Israel emerges in several ways: financial, military, and diplomatic. While most Americans assume that US foreign aid goes to help the poorest people in the poorest countries, in fact it is Israel (wealthier than a number of European Union member countries) that receives 25 percent of the entire US foreign aid budget. Since 1976, Israel has remained the highest recipient of US foreign aid in the world. The congressionally mandated aid comes to about $1.8 billion a year in military aid and $1.2 billion in economic aid, plus another $1 billion or so in miscellaneous grants, mostly in military supplies, from various US agencies. Tax-exempt contributions to Israel by private citizens bring the total of US aid to over $5 billion annually.

Israel is the only country allowed to spend part of its military aid funds (25 percent) on its own domestic arms industry; all other recipients of US military aid are required to use it to purchase US-manufactured weapons. This has helped Israel consolidate its own arms-exporting sector, some parts of which actually compete for export customers with US arms manufacturers. More directly, Israel has access to the most advanced weapons systems in the US arsenal, for purchase with US taxpayer assistance. The US defends Israel's refusal to sign the Nuclear Non-Proliferation Treaty, and has endorsed the principle of "strategic ambiguity" in which Israel refuses to officially acknowledge its widely known and documented nuclear capacity. Its arsenal of over 200 high-density nuclear bombs in the Dimona nuclear facility remains un-inspected.

During the Cold War, the US relied on Israel's military power as an extension of its own, with Israeli arms sales, military training, and backing of pro-US governments and pro-US anti-government guerrillas in countries from Mozambique and Angola to El Salvador, Chile, and Nicaragua. That "cat's paw" relationship consolidated the US–Israeli military ties that continue today. Most of the weapons Israel uses in the occupied territories, including Apache helicopter gunships, F-16 fighter bombers, wire-guided missiles, armored Caterpillar bulldozers used to demolish Palestinian houses, and others are all made in the US, and purchased from US manu-facturers with US military aid funds. Some of the weapons, such as the Merkava tanks, are joint products of Israel's domestic arms industry and US manufacturing technology.

Diplomatically, the US alone protects Israel in the United Nations and other international arenas and keeps it from being held accountable for its violations of international law. After 1967, the US patterns of opposing UN resolutions critical of Israel become more pronounced. Most of the US vetoes cast in the Security Council in the 1980s and '90s, and almost all of those cast since the end of the Cold War, have been to protect Israel. In the six years beginning in 2000, there were nine vetoes in the Security Council; eight of them were cast by the US to prevent the UN from criticizing Israel.

## Why was the Bush administration so much less involved than the Clinton administration in Israel– Palestine diplomacy?

In 2001, during the first months of its term and prior to September 11, the Bush administration adopted a policy of keeping up the high levels of aid to and diplomatic protection of Israel, while keeping their heads down and their hands off on peace talks. It wasn't terribly surprising—this was an administration whose top officials' own economic and political power was thoroughly enmeshed in the oil industry, with a long history of tight relations with oil-rich Arab states. The oil and stability legs of the Middle East policy triad were primary at first, although they were soon outweighed by the rise of the neoconservatives and Christian fundamentalists whose support for Israel was unequivocal.

Certainly the existing close US ties to Israel were strengthened during those pre-9/11 months of the Bush administration. But despite the continuity of $5 billion or so in military and economic aid, and the continued threat and/or use of UN vetoes and walk-outs to protect Israel in the United Nations, the Bush Middle East policy became known as "disengagement." Europe, Arab states, and others around the world began crying for "greater engagement," as if Washington's billions in aid, the protective vetoes, and the diplomatic privileging of Israel did not constitute intimate engagement; it was just a kind of engagement that did not include an active commitment to serious peace efforts. US diplomatic passivity, however, did not obscure the green light given to Israeli Prime Minister Ariel Sharon by the Bush administration to use a free hand against the civilian population of the occupied territories.

### *What has the George W. Bush administration's Middle East policy been all about?*

Immediately after the September 11, 2001, attacks, the Bush administration appeared to distance itself from Israel. Bush's need to maintain Arab and Islamic government support in the "war on terrorism" briefly trumped the intensity of the US's usual warm embrace of Israel, although the economic and strategic backing of Israel remained quietly unchanged. Fearing even greater distancing, Israeli spokespeople launched a near-frenzied campaign, claiming unparalleled unity with Americans as common victims of terrorism and common Arab/Islamic enemies. For a while that pressure campaign didn't change the rhetoric, and in November 2001 both Secretary of State Colin Powell and President Bush himself, at the UN General Assembly, paid significant attention to words the Palestinians and—more strategically—Arab govern-ments and their restive populations, wanted to hear. Bush's call for a "state of Palestine" and Powell's "the occupation must end" appeared to herald a new, maybe even close to even-handed, approach for US diplomacy.

But that relative evenhandedness was not to last. As it became less important to maintain the coalition in Afghanistan (since major cities under Taliban rule were already falling to the US and its allies), the tactical pendulum swung back, and Washington returned to a more public embrace of Israel and Prime Minister Ariel Sharon. This took the form of an announced intention to "re-engage" in the "peace process." The first messenger was General Anthony Zinni, whose two brief visits to the Middle East at the end of 2001 ended in failure. For a while the administration appeared unconcerned with the escalating violence, appearing to believe, against all evidence, that Palestine could burn, the supply of desperate young suicide bombers heading into Israel could remain unending, and yet the crisis would somehow stay contained.

But then, by about February 2002, Iraq reemerged as a central feature of US regional efforts. The stakes were rising; a new round of regional shuttle diplomacy was required to lay out the requirements and lay down the law to the US's Arab allies regarding support for a US attack on Iraq. General Zinni wasn't quite high enough in the administration hierarchy for this one, so into the breech stepped Vice President Dick Cheney, an experienced Middle East hand from his years as secretary of defense in the elder Bush's admini- stration. (Actually, Cheney's oil-driven loyalties were clear long before: as a member of the House of

Representatives, Cheney supported the 1981 sale of AWACS planes to Saudi Arabia, despite powerful Israeli opposition, and in 1979, he voted against the windfall profits tax on oil company revenues.)

In the wake of September 11, with dependent and already compliant Arab regimes virtually falling over each other to climb on board the Bush "anti-terrorism" train, the administration seemed to anticipate that Cheney's job would be effortless. Sure there might be some unease in the palaces over how to deal with Arab populations already raging about the rapidly deteriorating crisis in the West Bank and Gaza, but it was assumed that however much they twitched and weaseled, the US's Arab allies would stand reluctantly with Washington against Iraq.

As it turned out, it wasn't quite so easy. The Israeli–Palestinian conflict stood in the way. While there was little doubt that at the end of the day the Arab kings, emirs, princes, and presidents would indeed do as their patron ordered, public opinion throughout the Arab world had hardened not only against Israel and its occupation, but against Israel's global sponsor, the United States. Arab governments from Egypt to Jordan to Saudi Arabia and beyond, already facing severe crises of legitimacy, might do as they were told by the Bush administration, but they would pay a very high price domestically for their alliance with Washington. Israel's escalation in the occupied territories provided what seemed to provide an easy dodge for the Arab royals: "How can you even talk to us about supporting an invasion or overthrow campaign against Iraq when Palestine is burning and you are doing nothing?"

Some time before Cheney's Air Force Two took off, someone in Washington realized what was about to happen, so to avoid an embarrassment of the vice president, General Zinni was sent back to the region first. His mandate for Israel–Palestine had not changed, and there was virtually no chance he would "succeed," however that elusive word was defined, but that was okay. His real goal had far more to do with developments in Arab capitals than those in Tel Aviv and Ramallah, where he began a shadow shuttle. Zinni was Cheney's political cover. The vice president could now point to Zinni's shuttle to refute claims that the US was doing nothing for the Israeli–Palestinian crisis.

Washington's diplomatic "re-engagement" in the region was largely designed with war in Iraq, not peace in Israel–Palestine, in mind. As it turned out, the Iraq plan didn't work either; dependent Arab rulers were simply not willing to concede prematurely and risk further destabilization or even potential threats to their regimes. Cheney's trip fizzled, and the Bush spin operation focused on convincing audiences inside and outside Washington that the vice president's trip had never been intended to consolidate support for an attack on Iraq.

Then it was Secretary of State Powell's turn. Following Cheney's failed trip, the Bush administration called a brief time-out in the new game of diplomatic engagement. The press focused largely on the problems of the messenger. Was General Zinni simply too far down in the hierarchy to have the requisite clout with Sharon and/or Arafat? Would Bush send General Powell, ratcheting up the four-star factor? But what was largely left out of the debate was the reality that it was not the messenger, but the mandate that would determine the success or failure of the mission. Zinni failed not because he wasn't of high enough rank, but because he had no mandate to seriously dictate terms to Israel. As it turned out, neither did Powell. Two suicide bombings in late March, killing dozens of Israeli civilians inside Israel, raised the stakes; Washington clearly was going to respond.

But before any new US decision was announced, March 29, 2002, brought an unprecedented Israeli military offensive across the West Bank, carried out with mostly US-provided tanks, helicopter gunships, armored bulldozers, and F-16s punching into Ramallah, Bethlehem, Nablus, Jenin, Tulkarem, and tiny villages in between. The Israeli side at least looked like what UN Secretary General Kofi Annan called "a conventional war," even though it was the world-class Israeli army operating in civilian areas; Palestinian resistance, where there was any, was largely limited to small arms and homemade explosives.

At that point, Bush himself jumped into the fray, in a major speech in the White House Rose Garden on April 4. He announced he would send Secretary of State Powell to the region, and outlined a vision, if a bit skimpy and more than a bit blurry, of what a peaceful settlement might look like: "The outlines of a just settlement are clear: two states, Israel and Palestine, living side by side, in peace and security."

For long-term thinking, the words were all there: Israel must stop settlement activity, and "the occupation must end through withdrawal to secure and recognized boundaries…" Four days later Bush said he had told Sharon, "I expect there to be withdrawal without delay." The words were strong. The key action, though, was limited to sending Powell back to the region. There would be no real pressure on Israel: no cut in the billions in military aid, no brake on the pipeline of military equipment being used against civilians, no reversal of the Israel-backing veto in the Security Council preventing the deployment of international protection or even observer forces. Bush talked the talk of serious pressure, but he refused to walk the walk.

The real limits of Bush's intentions were made clear in the timetable. Powell would go to the region, but he would take his time getting there. When Powell arrived first in Morocco, the young king greeted him by asking, "Why are you here, why aren't you in Jerusalem?"

Powell's languid pace, from Morocco to Madrid, to Jordan, to Egypt, before arriving almost a week later in Jerusalem, provided what amounted to a week-long green light for Sharon's assault on the cities, villages, and especially refugee camps of the

West Bank. Yet, when Powell returned from his fruitless shuttle, President Bush welcomed him home with the claim that US goals had been met, that the trip was a success, that all was well with the world. It was an upside-down, Alice in Wonderland moment, with Bush then announcing straight-faced that "I do believe Ariel Sharon is a man of peace."

Israel's assault gradually wound down in some of the West Bank refugee camps, even as tensions mounted around Bethlehem's besieged Church of the Nativity and Arafat's tank-encircled presidential compound in Ramallah. But the goal of the Bush administration, the aim of Zinni's, Cheney's, and Powell's shuttles, as well as those of the underlings who took over when the top officials went home, had failed. The objective, to stabilize the region sufficiently so that Arab regimes could safely endorse a US military strike against Iraq without fearing domestic upheaval, had not been reached.

And at home, the Bush administration faced its first serious foreign policy challenge from the right. Christian fundamentalists and other components of the Republican Party's hard right edge moved into an even tighter embrace of Ariel Sharon's government, rejecting even Bush's rhetorical pretense of concern for Palestinian rights. Paul Wolfowitz, ardent pro-Israeli hawk and Bush's deputy chief of the Pentagon, was booed by tens of thousands of Christian "We stand with Israel" demonstrators when he had the audacity to mention in a brief aside that Palestinian children might be suffering too. The danger of a serious split within the Republican Party—with its farthest right wing and neoconservatives backing Israel, while the "moderates" clung to their traditional ties to big oil and the Arab regimes—loomed as a Texas-sized nightmare for the president.

By mid-summer, Iraq war fever was epidemic in Washington. Competing battle plans for diverse military operations were leaked by competing administration factions to competing newspapers. Powerful Republicans in Congress, the pages of the *New York Times*, the State Department, former Republican officials, even the Joint Chiefs of Staff hesitated about or even rejected the increasingly belligerent war cries of the Pentagon's civilian leadership. But as the debate about Iraq wore on, supplanting most other international stories on the front pages and the news shows, the crisis in Israel–Palestine continued with no end in sight. There was no US effort to craft new peace talks aimed at making real the president's rhetorical commitment to ending the occupation and creating an independent Palestinian state.

### *Where does US aid to Israel fit in the broader scheme of US foreign aid? Does the US provide aid to the Palestinians also?*

The US sends about $4 billion to Israel in military and economic aid every year, in addition to tax-exempt contributions. About $3 billion is mandated directly from Congress (the rest comes in smaller increments from specific US agencies) and amounts to about one-quarter of the entire US aid budget. US laws require that aid to Israel remain at least above Israel's international debt, thus insuring that US tax funds act as a guarantee of all Israeli loans. Israel is among only a tiny number of countries whose US aid allotments have remained steady even in recent years of economic slump.

Other US laws insure specific aid commitments to Israel as a result of the first Camp David process between Israel and Egypt. Under those arrangements, Egypt, with nearly 70 million people and a per capita annual income of $4,498, receives only about two-thirds of the funds allocated to Israel, the 27th wealthiest country in the world, with per capita income of about $23,800 for its approximately 6 million citizens.

In 2001, Israel itself requested that the apportion-ment of its US aid be shifted. Instead of the current balance of about $1.8 billion in military aid and $1.2 billion in economic assistance, the new plan called for an approximately ten percent reduction of economic aid, to be matched by a parallel increase in military aid. The goal would be, after ten years, to have Israel's entire aid allocation in the form of military assistance.

After the creation of the Palestinian Authority, the US provided some economic aid to the Pales-tinians. But unlike European and Japanese aid to the Palestinian Authority, or US aid to Israel, US financial support for Palestinians was provided only to non-governmental organizations working in the occupied territories—none directly to the PA. While the PA, like so many fully sovereign governments that the US supports, certainly has serious problems of corruption, bypassing it only insures the PA's continued weakness and inability to even begin to function as a government. After the election of Hamas to lead the PA's parliament and government in January 2006, the US orchestrated an international economic boycott of the PA, collectively punishing the entire Palestinian population.

### Didn't the US support creation of the Palestinian Authority? Why did the US treat it differently than the PLO, which Washington usually tried to undermine or sideline?

The Palestinian Authority was a product of the Oslo process, which began with the signing of the Israeli–Palestinian Declaration of Principles on the White House lawn in September 1993. While Oslo grew out of a secret diplomatic track initiated by Norway, the US quickly took over as the main sponsor, and acted as overseer of the process and, tacitly, patron of the Palestinian Authority itself.

The US saw the PA as a useful tool for accomplishing a key US goal: stability and normal-ization in the occupied Palestinian territories. The PA's authority was limited politically and geo-graphically, and derivative ultimately of Israeli power. Israel viewed the PA largely as an agency that would be responsible for organizing social and economic life in the Palestinian territories, including schools, health, welfare, etc., thus alleviating Israel's obligation under the Geneva Conventions to take care of the lives of the occupied population, but without allowing any real power to the Palestinian Authority. Later, when Palestinian resistance to the occupation escalated, and especially with the emergence of suicide bombing attacks inside Israel, both Israel and the US began to view the PA as a security agency—not to protect the lives and safety of Palestinians living under occupation, but to prevent any attacks on Israel. It was as though the Palestinian Authority was to serve as a surrogate for Israel's own power—assigned the job of keeping Palestinians under control.

Unlike the PA, the PLO was a product of the Palestinians themselves. While it was initially under the control of the Arab governments, the PLO was from the beginning made up of indigenous Palestinian resistance organizations, and its own history was that of a nationalist movement fighting against an occupying power. Its means of fighting, both military and diplomatic, were similar to those of many other liberation movements, particularly during the anti-colonial wars of the 1960s and '70s. Yet the US, as was true in so many other cases of liberation movements fighting against US allies, identified the PLO as a "terrorist" organization, the same brush that the US used to tar the African National Congress and its leader, Nelson Mandela (Mandela remained on a US list of "undesirable South Africans" until 2003). As a result, despite UN and widespread international recognition of the PLO as the sole legitimate representative of the Palestinian people, the US refused until late1988 to recognize or negotiate with the organization. Instead, the US backed Israeli efforts to anoint various non-PLO Palestinian leaders and notables as the "acceptable" Palestinians, and US-led diplomatic efforts failed.

### *If not the US, then who else should be at the center of Middle East diplomacy?*

The United Nations should be the nucleus of a new diplomatic process. The UN created the State of Israel; Israel's occupation of the West Bank, Gaza, and East Jerusalem violates numerous UN resolutions; and the Israeli—Palestinian conflict has global significance and thus should be addressed by an international body. Also, the US-orchestrated diplomacy has failed. As Brazilian President Luis Inácio Lula da Silva told the opening plenary of the General Assembly in September 2006, "Middle Eastern issues have always been dealt with exclusively by the great powers. They have achieved no solution so far. One might then ask: is it not time to call a broad, UN-sponsored Conference, with the participation of countries of the region and others that could contribute through their capacity and successful experience, in living peacefully with differences?"

UN resolutions, not a US-created "road map," set the terms of what UN-led diplomacy would look like: an international peace conference under the auspices of the Security Council, or indeed the General

Assembly (a far more representative UN agency), and involving all the parties to the conflict, including Israel, the Palestinians, the Arab states, as well as Europe, the US, and the rest of the international community. The conference should be based on all relevant UN resolutions and internationally guaranteed rights for all parties, and the goal should be to bring about an end to occupation of the West Bank, Gaza, and East Jerusalem and to create an independent Palestinian state. Specific issues to be resolved would include an end to occupation, meaning an end to house demolitions, curfews, closures, seizures of water resources, and other practices; abolition of settlements; recognition and implementation of the right of return for Palestinian refugees; and security guarantees for both Israelis and Palestinians to live without fear of violence.

### Didn't the United Nations create the State of Israel? Why didn't it create a State of Palestine too? Why doesn't it now?

After World War II, with the British eager to give up their League of Nations Mandate over Palestine, the United Nations General Assembly took responsibility for the conflict-riven area. The local indigenous population was angry about the influx of European Jewish settlers, whose numbers rose dramatically as the US and Britain refused to allow large-scale immigration of European Jews escaping, or later having barely survived, the Holocaust. For many of those refugees, British-controlled Palestine was their only possible refuge, whether it was their first-choice destination or not. (Far more European Jewish refugees wanted to come to the US, where many had families.) Fighting escalated between the indigenous Palestinian population and the European settlers, and the British occupation soldiers became targets of both. The UN Special Commission on Palestine, or UNSCOP, recommended that Palestine be divided into two states, one Jewish and one Arab.

The November 29, 1947 resolution partitioning Palestine apportioned 55 percent of Mandate Palestine to the new State of Israel, leaving 45 percent for a future Palestinian state. The Zionist leaders accepted partition, though in private several indicated their intention to expand the new state to include all of Palestine. But Palestinians were opposed to the partition. At the time of the UN resolution, Jews in Palestine constituted just about 30 percent of the population, and they owned only 6 percent of the land. Given that, it was seen by Palestinians, by many others in the Middle East, and many around the world as a massive injustice for the Jewish population, almost all of them recent settlers, to be granted more than half the land. In fact, the land the UN selected to become the Jewish state included within it over 450,000 Palestinian Arabs; the number of Jews in the area designated to become a Palestinian Arab state was tiny.

The Palestinian state never came into existence. The Israeli Jewish state did, of course, and by the end of the 1948 conflict it had taken over 78 percent of the land, far more than the 55 percent actually allocated to it by the United Nations.

In fact, no one seriously consulted the Palestinians themselves. While most were strongly opposed to partition, the relevant opposition, on the world stage, came not from the Palestinians but from the Arab governments in the region. They were opposed also, though in general they had little interest in defending the rights of the Palestinians. As soon as Israel declared its independence, their armies moved to oppose the well-armed Zionist militias, but they were soon defeated. Overnight, 750,000 Palestinians were made refugees.

Once hostilities ended, Israel was recognized as an independent state (though it still has never officially acknowledged its borders). Egypt and Jordan were in control of the now separate parts of Arab Palestine that remained, and Palestinian independence was not on any international agenda.

Since 1967, when the US–Israeli special relationship was solidified into a powerful military-economic alliance, the US has consistently protected Israel diplomatically, including keeping the question of Palestinian independence and an end to occupation for the most part off the enforceable agenda of the UN, especially the agenda of the UN Security Council.

## *Why is Israel so often criticized in the UN? Aren't other countries just as guilty of human rights violations?*

There are many countries in the United Nations that commit human rights violations. Israel is criticized by the international community more than many other countries because its violations of Palestinian human rights are also violations of international law and a host of specific UN resolutions. This is because the specific violations often targeted by UN resolutions—building settlements, demolition of Palestinian houses, military attacks on civilians, closures, and curfews, etc.—all take place in the context of a military occupation that is itself illegal. Other countries—Algeria, Saudi Arabia, Egypt, Colombia, Uzbekistan, and many more—commit massive human rights violations against their own population, but only Israel carries out those actions against a population that is supposed to be protected by the Geneva Conventions, which guarantee safety for people living under occupation. In addition, Israel's claim to be an enlightened "Western" democracy means that it holds itself up to what are perceived by many as the highest standards in the world; its violations are therefore all the more stark. And finally, part of the reason for the seemingly repetitive resolutions challenging Israel's human rights violations against the Palestinians lies with the consistent US actions designed to prevent implementation, and therefore protect Israel from the consequences of its violations. If Israel was forced to comply, new resolutions covering old ground would be unnecessary.

*What is the role of the UN in the Middle East these days? Why isn't the UN in charge of the overall peace process?*

In 1991, in issuing invitations for participation in the Madrid peace conference, the US accepted Israel's demand that the United Nations be excluded from participation in the conference, allowing instead only the symbolic presence of a single representative of the secretary-general, who was not allowed to speak. With the beginning of the Oslo peace process, the US moved even further, forcing the United Nations to pull back from longstanding positions, and sidelining the role of the global organization.

Since the Oslo process took hold, the US largely kept the United Nations out of the loop on Israel–Palestine diplomacy. In August 1994, then US Ambassador to the UN Madeleine Albright introduced a letter outlining Washington's goals for the General Assembly. The overall thrust was essentially to remove the issues of Arab–Israeli relations, and especially the question of Palestine, from the UN's political agenda, by claiming that the bilateral Israeli–Palestinian negotiations of the Madrid and Oslo processes had rendered UN involvement irrelevant except for economic and development assistance. Almost all past resolutions were identified as needing to be "consolidated... improved... or eliminated." The US campaign also demanded that any UN concerns over the fundamental questions of refugees, settlements, territorial sovereignty, and the status of Jerusalem "should be dropped, *since these issues are now under negotiations by the parties themselves.*" (Emphasis added.) The sad irony, of course, was that under the terms of Oslo those were the precise questions not under negotiation, because they were designated "final status" issues that would not come under consideration for five or seven years.

That pattern continued. In October 2000, when fourteen out of fifteen members of the UN Security Council voted to condemn Israel's excessive force against civilians, it was the US alone that abstained. Then US Ambassador Richard Holbrooke threatened to veto any further resolution.

At the time of Israel's re-occupation of Jenin in March 2002, the Security Council was able to convince US diplomats to accept a resolution calling for a UN investigation of the catastrophic crisis that had laid waste the city and killed 52 Palestinians and 23 Israeli soldiers. Israel initially agreed, but when Israel soon withdrew its approval for the fact-finding team, the US backed their rejection and refused to allow the Council or the secretary-general to enforce the resolution. The fact-finding team was disbanded. The General Assembly, however, responded to the developments by reconvening in Emergency Session to pass its own resolution calling for the secretary-general to prepare a report based on other sources, primarily international human rights organizations.

In July 2002, at the height of Israel's re-occupation of Palestinian cities, the new US Ambassador John

Negroponte told a closed Security Council meeting that a proposed resolution condemning Israel was unhelpful and that the US would oppose it if it came to a vote. But he then went much further, telling the Council that in the future the US would only consider resolutions concerning the Middle East that explicitly condemned Palestinian terrorism, and named and denounced several specific Palestinian organizations. There was no such demand that all future resolutions equally condemn Israeli military or settler violence.

But the General Assembly's response to the Council's deadlock raises the possibility of a broader role for the UN's most democratic component. Under longstanding UN precedent, if the Council (which is the most powerful, but the least democratic, part of the UN because of the veto held by the five permanent members) is deemed deadlocked, the General Assembly may take up issues that would ordinarily be limited to Council jurisdiction. That may make possible Assembly initiatives on issues such as international protection for Palestinians living under occupation (something repeatedly vetoed by the US), or ultimately the creation of an entirely new diplomatic process, perhaps similar to that proposed by Brazilian President Lula in September 2006.

### *Why is Israel isolated from Arab countries in the region and in the UN and other international forums?*

Some of Israel's isolation reflects antagonism from neighboring countries, and some of it stems from

Israel's own orientation and self-definition in the world. At the time the State of Israel was created, there was already wide-spread antagonism among Palestinians and in surrounding Arab countries toward the large and rapid influx of European Jews. While European Jewish settlement had gone on since the 1880s, the numbers vastly increased in the 1930s and '40s, as Jews escaping the Holocaust, and those who survived it, were rejected by their first-choice countries of refuge, the US and Britain, and instead turned to British-ruled Palestine, where the UK kept the door mostly open. Significant loss of land and political power for the indigenous Arab population resulted. Arabs, both Palestinians and others, resented being forced to pay the price for European anti-Semitism and the Holocaust, in which they had played little significant role.

At the same time, the pre-state Zionist organizations and later Israeli government leaders viewed themselves as squarely part of the Western, Euro-American part of the world. Despite being located in the heart of the Arab Middle East, Israel positioned itself as a "civilized," "Western" outpost—explicitly so in early pleas of support sent to British colonial leaders such as Cecil Rhodes—in a foreign, "uncivilized" part of the world. From the beginning of their state-building project, Israeli officials oriented their economic, political, and cultural policies toward Europe and the US, rather than making efforts to cultivate ties with their neighbors.

After the 1967 war, when Israel occupied the last

22 percent of historic Palestine as well as occupying Syria's Golan Heights, Egypt's Sinai Peninsula, and still later a wide swathe of southern Lebanon, Arab anger increased still further. The view of Israel for an entire new Arab generation—Palestinians growing up under occupation, Syrians dismayed at their government's inability to reclaim its lost territory, Egyptians dismayed by their military defeat and the occupation of Egypt's Sinai peninsula, and more—was shaped by the harsh reality of occupation. And Arab anger toward, and rejection of, Israel increased. In 1968, the Arab League voted to reject diplomatic and economic ties with Israel. Even earlier, Arab countries had put in place an economic boycott that prohibited trade with Israel. Egypt broke ranks with the rest of the Arab world in normalizing relations with Israel after the Camp David Accords of 1979, and faced years of ostracism within the Arab League. The Arab boycott faded with the signing of the Oslo Accords in 1993, and Jordan and Israel agreed to full diplomatic and economic relations in 1994. Other countries, including Oman and Morocco, established various levels of trade and economic ties with Israel.

In the United Nations, certain privileges and positions, including rotating membership in the Security Council, are determined within the regional groups of the General Assembly. Composition of the groups, determined at the height of the Cold War, are partly geographic and partly political (i.e., Eastern Europe and Western Europe are in different regional groups). To protest its occupation and policies toward Palestinians, Israel was excluded from participation in the Asian Group that includes the surrounding Arab countries. In 2000, Secretary-General Kofi Annan orchestrated a campaign within the UN to have Israel accepted by WEOG, the Western European and Others Group, which also includes the United States and Canada. In recent years, civil society organizations led by Palestinian non-governmental organizations and the UN-based International Coordinating Network on Palestine called for campaigns of "BDS"—boycotts, divestment, and sanctions—to bring nonviolent pressure to bear on Israel to end its occupation and implement Palestinian rights.

*Since Jordan's population is about two-thirds Palestinian and there are 21 other Arab countries, why do the Palestinians insist on having a new state of their own?* Palestine's origins, and its identity as a distinct region within the broader Arab world, go back thousands of years. Like that of most of the countries of the Arab world, Palestine's specific identity as a modern nation-state emerged only in the context of colonial rule. British and French diplomats first created Palestine's modern borders, along with those of Syria, Lebanon, Iraq, Jordan, Kuwait, Saudi Arabia, and other Gulf statelets, when they divided up the Arab portion of the defeated Ottoman Empire in 1922. Some of those newly identified states became independent; others remained under colonial or later French or British

Mandate authority. But in all of these newly created countries, newly "national" identity emerged within the local populations. (Iraq, whose national identity reaches back to ancient Ur and Sumeria, already had such a national consciousness.)

For Palestinians, national identity was first linked to the land itself. It was *their* land; their grandparents and great-grandparents and on to the incalculable past had farmed this same land, these same olive trees. It was very specific. National dialects, customs, cultural norms, etc., all developed in particular and identifiably Palestinian forms. The notion of being transferred to another country, just because they speak the same language, even before the beginning of the modern Arab nation-states, was unacceptable. The equivalent would be expecting seventh- or eighth-generation Americans to accept forcible transfer to Australia, or Britain, or even Canada, simply because they speak the same language. Perhaps a more exact comparison, taken from US history, was the forced transfer of Native American tribes from one shrinking reservation to another, on the theory that they could live anywhere just as well as in their indigenous territory. The 4,000 deaths resulting from the Cherokees' forced removal from Georgia along the "Trail of Tears" in 1838–39 was only one such example.

In 1982, then Defense Minister Ariel Sharon developed a "Jordan is Palestine" plan designed to legitimate the idea of forcible transfer of Palestinians out of the West Bank and Gaza, perhaps out of Israel itself, into "their" alleged homeland in Jordan. The campaign never took off, and by 1988, at the height of the first intifada, Jordan's King Hussein announced he was severing the formal sponsorship of West Bank institutions to ensure that there would be no confusion about the right of Palestinians to their own state in Palestine.

What the Palestinians in the twenty-first century want is not a "new" state, but recognition of the independence and sovereignty of what is left of their old nation, which was never allowed to become independent.

### Don't the Arab countries want to destroy Israel and drive the Jews into the sea?

Unlike in Europe, anti-Semitism was not a long-standing component of popular or elite culture in the Arab world. During the Spanish Inquisition, fleeing Jews famously found refuge in the Arab countries, particularly in North Africa.

In the period leading up to the creation of the State of Israel and the 1948 war that accompanied it, many Arabs both inside Palestine and in the surrounding Arab countries believed it would be possible to prevent the creation of a Jewish state, a self-proclaimed enclave of Europe and America in the heart of the Arab Middle East. Across the region people opposed the creation of the state, believing it unjust to the indigenous Palestinians, and governments opposed it largely from fear that a powerful, western-backed Israel would represent a serious threat to their countries' own economic, strategic, and political interests.

The token Arab armies that entered Palestine in 1948 were soundly defeated by the smaller but far superior Israeli military. They were defeated again in 1967 when Israel's first strikes destroyed the entire Egyptian and Jordanian air forces before either country could scramble a single plane. Since that time, despite further wars, tensions, and continuing occupation, Arab governments have largely come to terms with the existence of Israel in their midst; many are eager to consolidate business and financial links with the far wealthier, far more powerful, far better-positioned Israeli economy. If popular opinion were not so strongly against such normalization, there is little doubt that virtually all the Arab governments would be lining up to exchange ambassadors with Tel Aviv.

Since the beginning of the first intifada, or uprising, in 1987, and especially since the collapse of Oslo negotiations and the beginning of the second intifada in 2000, regional anger toward Israel for its treatment of Palestinians living under occupation has skyrocketed. The emergence in the mid-1990s of Arabic-language satellite television stations (most notably Qatar's al-Jazeera, along with Abu Dhabi's al-Arabiyya TV) transformed the level of outrage. While most Arabs long knew and opposed Israeli occupation, seeing televised coverage of the day-to-day humiliations, killings, and episodes of extreme violence that are endemic to military occupation brought that opposition to new and angry levels. But still, the dominant opinion in the Arab world focuses on ending Israel's occupation and creating an independent Palestinian state. The supposedly iconic call to "drive the Jews into the sea" was never an accepted political slogan.

### How does Israel see its role in the Middle East region?

The pre-state Zionist leadership deliberately crafted an identity for the new State of Israel that was oriented toward Europe, America, and the West. This was partly a tactical effort to win backing from one or another of the colonial powers; to do so, the putative Israelis had to convince their would-be sponsors of their potential value as a surrogate for European, American, Russian, or Roman Catholic sponsors. But it also reflected the personal worldview of those same leaders; while early Zionist colonies in Palestine were largely agricultural, most Jewish settlers would have been far more at home in Paris, London, or New York than in the Middle Eastern hills or desert.

Throughout the Cold War, Israel deliberately shaped its position as a junior partner, or surrogate, for US military and strategic reach. Cynical remarks about Israel as the "fifty-first state" reflected the familiarity of the US–Israeli bond. For Washington, while Cold War–driven strategic considerations were the main driving force behind the embrace of Israel, a powerful component was the sense that "Israelis are like us." There was more than a hint of racism in this assessment; it was designed to distinguish Israel from its neighbors. However close our ties with Egypt or Saudi Arabia, official Washington thinking went, they're still Arabs, they're not quite "like us." Official and other influential Israeli voices consistently promoted that racist view. The irony, of course, was that increasing numbers of Israeli Jews had immigrated or were descended from communities in the Arab world (or Iran or Turkey), despite the tendency of many to take on the widespread Israeli identification with Europe more than with their own Middle Eastern languages and cultures. But racism and history combined in Israel to ensure the continuing domination of Ashkenazi, or white European, Jewish leadership in Israeli government, business, and intellectual circles, making it easier for US officials and business leaders accustomed to dealing with Europeans, not with Arabs.

### What role does the European Union play in the conflict? Why doesn't it do more?

Europe has generally maintained a nuanced position, preserving strong economic and political ties to Israel, while expressing firm opposition to Israeli settlements in the occupied Palestinian territories and recognition of how those settlements violate the Geneva Conventions, numerous United Nations resolutions, and other instruments of international law. The Euro-Israeli Association Accord, for instance, privileges European–Israeli trade by removing tariffs for all goods made in Israel. The Accord has been the basis of a challenge by the European Union to Israel's practice of labeling goods produced in Israeli settlements in the occupied territories as "made in

Israel" and including them as tariff-free, in violation of the accord's provisions. But the unwillingness of some European countries, most notably Germany and the Netherlands, to criticize Israel openly has prevented the EU from reaching the necessary unanimity to hold Israel accountable for those violations.

While Europe was invited to the 1991 Madrid peace talks, it was functionally excluded; the US alone set the terms, developed the agenda, and recruited the participants. During the Oslo process, the European Union was called on to pay much of the cost, but remained excluded from serious involvement in the actual diplomacy. European governments throughout the Clinton era appeared to acquiesce to US domination over Middle East diplomacy. Despite his claimed commitment to "assertive multilateralism" as the bulwark of his foreign policy, Clinton never relinquished even partial control of the Israeli–Palestinian peace process to the Europeans—and Europe never pushed very hard for a seat at the table. In the mid-1990s, the European Commission drafted a long critique of US policy toward the Israeli–Palestinian conflict, and especially of Europe's exclusion from the process. But the report concluded with the statement that nothing in it should be taken as a "challenge to US leadership" on the issue, thus largely vitiating the critique's impact.

When George Bush was elected, European diplomats were wary of the seeming disinterest of this oil industry-oriented administration in the explosive region. By summer 2001, the EU was already moving in where Washington feared to tread. European diplomats helped negotiate an end to Israel's two-day tank-led occupation of the Palestinian town of Beit Jala in August. The EU's security chief, Javier Solana, shuttled between Israeli and Palestinian officials, attempting to broker a new cease-fire. Then, when a new crisis erupted after Israel shut down the Orient House, long the Palestinians' diplomatic center in East Jerusalem, Europe, in particular Germany, moved in. Even the White House acknowledged that the Israeli action represented an "escalation" of the occupation. German Foreign Minister Joschka Fischer happened to be in the region at the time, and quickly moved to the center of the diplomatic effort to reopen the Palestinian offices.

After urging Israel to reopen the Orient House, Fischer invited the parties to meet in Berlin to open a new dialogue. But he undermined his own position with a careful bow to what he called "the American prerogative" in Middle East diplomacy. His initiative might have borne fruit; but just a few days later the terrorist attacks of September 11 occurred, and Europe pulled back.

Only months later, when the post-9/11 global diplomatic impasse slowly began to crumble, did Europe begin to revive its cautious efforts. With Israel's violent re-occupation of Palestinian cities in the spring of 2002, most of the European-funded security infrastructure of the Palestinian Authority (police stations, police cars, etc.) were destroyed by Israeli soldiers. Israel made clear its expectation that

Europe, not Israel itself, should be expected to cough up the funds to rebuild the shattered infrastructure.

In early 2006, Europe signed on to the US-orchestrated boycott of the Palestinian Authority following the election of Hamas as the dominant party in the PA. Many European parliamentarians, as well as large majorities of Europe's populations, expressed serious concern about at least the humanitarian, if not necessarily the political, consequences of such drastic actions, but US pressure won out. During the Israeli escalation that began that same summer, Europe criticized Israel's violations of the Geneva Conventions and other international covenants in its collective punishment of the Palestinians, and especially in the Israeli military's destruction of much of the Palestinian civilian infrastructure, such as Gaza's sole electricity-generating plant, which was destroyed in June 2006. Europe offered on several occasions to pay to rebuild that infrastructure, but its financial generosity was not matched by a willingness to take the necessary political steps to halt the Israeli assault.

# PART III

RECENT HISTORY: RISING VIOLENCE

*Why did violence break out again in 2000?*
*What is this second "intifada," and how is it different*
*from the first intifada of 1987–1993?*

The second uprising, or intifada, began in September 2000. While the immediate spark was General Ariel Sharon's walk on the Muslim holy site, the Haram al-Sharif in East Jerusalem, the uprising's real origins had far more to do with the failed peace process and the dashed hopes and deteriorating lives of Palestinians living under occupation, than with any particular provocation.

The second intifada came seven years after the first intifada ended with the signing of the Oslo accords in 1993. Oslo did not bring about the actual goals of the first intifada—the end of occupation and creation of an independent Palestinian state—but it did hold out the hope that the new diplomatic "peace process" would lead inexorably to such a result. So the nonviolent uprising—including the mass mobilizations, daily commercial strikes, widespread tax resistance, and stone-throwing children that characterized the first intifada—came to a halt with the signing of Oslo's "Declaration of Principles" on the White House lawn.

Seven long years followed, in which the "peace process" ground on with little result. Especially after the collapse of the Israeli–Palestinian summit sponsored by President Bill Clinton at Camp David in August 2000, Palestinians faced the unfortunate reality that Oslo's diplomacy had been much more about "process" than about peace. Palestinians' living conditions and economy had all seriously deteriorated throughout the Oslo years. Israel's military occupation had become increasingly harsh: closures preventing Palestinians from entering Israel were expanded to prevent travel within and between the West Bank and Gaza; military checkpoints proliferated throughout the "Swiss cheese–style" maze of Israeli control and partial Palestinian authority; house demolitions continued; and settlement construction nearly doubled throughout the occupied territories since Oslo.

The second intifada was the response to those lost hopes. Initially it took similar forms to the first intifada—mass protests in the streets against Israeli military checkpoints surrounding Palestinian cities, including children and youths throwing stones at the tanks and armored vehicles, characterized the first weeks' mobilization. But the Israeli response was far more brutal than it had been during the first intifada; the stone-throwing protesters the day after Sharon's provocative visit to the Haram al-Sharif were met with withering fire, killing four and wounding hundreds on the steps and even inside the mosques. The Israeli military immediately began using live fire and tank-fired weapons where once tear gas and rubber bullets might have been used first, and soon helicopter gunships and US-supplied F-16 fighter bombers became regular parts of the Israeli arsenal in the occupied territories.

By March 2002, Amnesty International reported over 1,000 Palestinians had been killed; more than 200 of them were children.

In response, Palestinians changed their tactics. The mass street demonstrations largely ended as the lethal price exacted by the Israelis for marches and stone-throwing rose. Instead, small armed Palestinian factions took over in challenging the Israeli military occupation forces. Since the Oslo process had created the Palestinian Authority, there were now Palestinian police and security forces armed with rifles and Kalashnikovs, and they used their arms both to protect Palestinian demonstrators and civilians, and sometimes to challenge directly the checkpoints and Israeli soldiers. One result was that killing on both sides escalated—but the deaths and injuries were disproportionately Palestinian (about four times as many), and initially the Israeli victims were almost all soldiers and settlers inside the occupied territories.

As the intifada settled into a kind of war of attrition, 24-hour shoot-to-kill curfews were imposed on Palestinian cities and villages for long periods, imprisoning people in their homes and bringing to an end the mass public participation in the streets that had characterized the first intifada.

**What was the "road map" that President Bush and British Prime Minister Tony Blair, on the eve of the Iraq war, seemed so convinced would end the Israeli–Palestinian conflict?**

The "road map" was a negotiating plan created by a diplomatic foursome—the US, Russia, the European Union, and the United Nations—led by the US and known as the Quartet. The group came together in August 2002, at the height of the international crisis that resulted from Israel's re-occupation of Palestinian cities in the West Bank and Gaza Strip. The road map was designed, ostensibly, to be presented to the Israelis and Palestinians in a more or less take-it-or-leave-it fashion, to impose on the two sides an internationally sanctioned resolution of the conflict.

But that was before the Bush administration began its attempt to redraw the map of the Middle East through its invasion of Iraq. The overthrow of the regime in Baghdad, the sacking of Iraq's cities, destroying much of its ancient history, and the devastation brought to the civilian population of the country have dramatically reshaped regional politics, in ways still not fully apparent. Despite the Bush administration's claims of victory in Iraq, the new Middle East remained occupied and violent. The road map's goals were largely sidelined.

But while the road map's relevance as a diplomatic strategy was limited, the goals specified in it were significant. Unlike the Oslo process, the Quartet's road map specifically identified the objective of ending the occupation, as well as engaging in a negotiating process to create some version of an independent Palestinian state and provide for Israeli security. It even set out timetables—the first phase was supposed to be completed by May 2003. In that period, Palestinians were supposed to declare and observe a unilateral cease-fire leading to the end of the intifada, reopen security cooperation, recognize Israel's right to exist in peace and security, appoint an "empowered" prime minister (this designed to undermine President Yasir Arafat), and begin drafting a constitution that would be subject to the Quartet's approval. Israel, in that same period, was supposed to allow Palestinian officials (only officials) to move from place to place inside the occupied territories, improve the humanitarian situation, end attacks on civilians and demolitions of homes, and pay the Palestinians the tax revenues due them. More importantly, Israel was also to immediately close the new settlement "outposts" erected since Sharon came to power in March 2001, and, also as part of phase one, to freeze all settlement activity. The road map did not require Israel to dismantle existing settlements, all of which are illegal under international law, but only to freeze further growth. Even that limited goal was never achieved.

In fact, even before the public announcement of the road map, the Palestinians (though not their Israeli counterparts) were already well on their way toward implementing the requirements: particularly through the sidelining of Yasir Arafat through the US-imposed selection of Mahmoud Abbas, known as Abu Mazen, as prime minister, with no popular election and little attention paid to Palestinian public opinion on the matter. The first phase was supposed to end in May 2003, but by that time Israel had moved only cosmetically against a few settlement "outposts," and actually escalated the actions against Palestinians supposedly prohibited under phase one: curfews; attacks on and killing of Palestinian civilians; demolition of Palestinian homes and property; destruction of Palestinian institutions and infrastructure; and settlement growth. In consequence, violence against Israelis, both soldiers and civilians, continued as well. In the second phase, there was supposed to be the "option" of creating a "provisional" Palestinian state in 2003, with temporary borders. Only after the Quartet approved each step would the final phase be reached, supposedly resulting eventually in negotiations on permanent status issues such as borders, refugees, Jerusalem, and settlements.

There were numerous serious problems and deficiencies in the road map. From its first phase on, it failed to achieve any of its major objectives, and certainly did not make any progress toward an end to the occupation and the establishment of an independent, sovereign, and viable State of Palestine.

The road map's failure was predictable. Beyond its omissions of key internationally recognized rights and its lack of specificity, there was a larger problem. The so-called Quartet was not really a four-part partnership, but more like a solo act with three back-up singers; US power easily dominated the other three. And because the rules of the Quartet dictated that decisions were made by consensus, the US had what amounted to a veto.

The first evidence came in December 2002, when the final language of the road map was completed. The Bush administration, acting in concert with Israeli wishes, announced that the text would not be made public until after the Israeli elections weeks later. After the victory of General Sharon's right-wing Likud-led coalition, announcement was delayed again until a cabinet was chosen. Once the Israeli cabinet was in place, another delay was announced until "the situation" in Iraq was resolved. Each delay allowed Israel to further consolidate its occupation. On the eve of the Iraq war, in early March 2003, faced with rising British anti-war sentiment that included anger at the perceived US—British abandonment of the Israeli—Palestinian conflict, Prime Minister Tony Blair insisted on a joint US—British announcement of the road map as soon as the newly appointed Palestinian prime minister had taken office.

But with war in Iraq raging, the road map dropped off the agenda again. By early April, General Sharon's government announced, with little fanfare and no response from the US or the other partners of the Quartet, that Israel had fourteen "reservations" on the terms of the road map, and if they were not accepted Israel would walk away from the negotiations.

The Israeli position also focused on keeping the US in charge, sidelining any potential influence of the other Quartet members: the UN, Russia, and the EU. Israel raised particular concern regarding the one area where the Quartet as a whole was supposed to play a key role, in approving Palestinian and Israeli compliance with the road map before moving on to the next phase. "We believe that the US has a dominant and leading role in this process and accordingly the supervision mechanism should be led by the Americans," the Israeli government said. "The Quartet may assist the process by supporting the American effort, but it cannot judge on issues such as determining goals for progress, judging on the transition from one phase to the next or addressing security issues."

On March 14, Bush announced his personal commitment to the road map. That same day, US National Security Advisor Condoleezza Rice convened a meeting with Jewish leaders to reassure them that American support for Israel was not in danger. "We will lead the process and not the Europeans," she told them. "We know you are worried about the Quartet, but we're in the driver's seat," she said. She was right. Neither the United Nations nor any of the other Quartet members were even invited to attend the June 2003 Aqaba summit heralding the road map. And the "international monitoring team" announced at the summit was solely an American creation, to be staffed by CIA and Pentagon officers and headed by a Bush administration official.

### Did the road map have any potential to actually bring about a new peace process?

For George Bush and for Tony Blair, the road map became a convenient way to try to convince the Arab world that even as they attacked Iraq they were still concerned about ending the Israeli–Palestinian conflict—without having to do anything to make it real. With the EU, Russia, and especially the UN (which should have been in the position of power in any international negotiations) unable and/or unwilling to challenge US domination of the process, the road map and its sponsors were unlikely to find a just solution to the crisis.

At the much-hyped Aqaba summit on June 24, 2003, Abu Mazen dutifully repeated the words the Bush administration had demanded: the armed intifada must end. Sharon, for his part, spoke only of closing "unauthorized" outposts—a far cry from the road map's official requirement for the closing of all settlements ("authorized" or not) established since March 2001. All settlements in the occupied territories, whether "authorized" by the Israeli government or not, were and are of course illegal under international law. President Bush, who also spoke of "unauthorized outposts" in his Aqaba speech, echoed Sharon's limited interpretation.

In its response to the December 2002 draft of the road map, the Israeli government had stated, "the purpose of the road map should be an end to the conflict... rather than an end to the 'occupation.'" That definition would entail making significant aspects of Israel's occupation permanent, ignoring the rights of Palestinian refugees and relegating them to permanent exile; reducing what was supposed to be a viable, independent Palestinian state to "certain attributes of sovereignty"; enforcing an end to

Palestinian resistance—and calling such a militarily driven solution an "end to the conflict."

Throughout the years in which the road map was ostensibly in operation, Israel continued to create new "facts on the ground." That term, long used by Israeli officials themselves, refers to actions that change the realities in the occupied territories—to Israel's benefit, and to the detriment of the Palestinians. Most often it has referred to such actions as the construction or expansion of settlements and the building of the Apartheid Wall.

Under international law it is always illegal for an occupying power, such as Israel in the Palestinian territories, to do anything to change conditions within occupied areas. In a spring 2006 report, the UN's Special Rapporteur for Human Rights John Dugard stated that "Israel is in violation of major Security Council and General Assembly resolutions dealing with unlawful territorial change and the violation of human rights, has failed to implement the 2004 Advisory Opinion of the International Court of Justice and should accordingly be subjected to international sanctions. Instead the Palestinian people have been subjected to possibly the most rigorous form of international sanctions imposed in modern times."

He acknowledged the failure of the road map and the Quartet, while calling for "creative diplomacy... that will enable Israel and the Palestinian Authority to resume negotiations for a peaceful settlement and respect for human rights." But, he went on,

Unfortunately the United States is unprepared to play the role of peace facilitator. This leaves the EU and the UN as the obvious honest brokers between Israelis and Palestinians. Whether either of these bodies can play this role while remaining part of the Quartet is questionable. The image of both the EU and the UN has suffered substantially among Palestinians as a result of the Quartet's apparent support for economic isolation, under the direction of the United States.... However, they remain the bodies most likely to achieve peace and promote human rights in the region. In these circumstances both bodies should seriously consider whether it is in the best interests of peace and human rights in the region for them to seek to find a peaceful solution through the medium of the Quartet.

At the same time, then UN Secretary-General Kofi Annan raised the possibility of a new diplomatic campaign outside the failed Quartet, saying "the UN and the other members of the international community are, for the moment, working through the Quartet, but it is not excluded that, down the line, maybe other broader initiatives may be necessary." Such a new initiative might take the form of a new UN-sponsored international peace conference, based on the political call of the 2002 Beirut Arab Summit Declaration, only at a global level instead of regional. Unlike the limited mandate of the so-called road map (which did not stop Israel's continued expansion of settlements or construction of the land-grabbing separation wall) such a conference, if successful, would have to be based on an unequivocal end to Israeli occupation, a just solution for Palestinian refugees based on the international law-based right of return and UN Resolution 194, and equal rights for all. Such a result would be the only basis for a just and lasting peace throughout the region.

*These developments happened after the famous 1993 handshake on the White House lawn. Wasn't that supposed to end the conflict between Israel and the Palestinians?*

The famous handshake between then Israeli Prime Minister Yitzhak Rabin and Palestinian leader Yasir Arafat, under the gentle urging of President Bill Clinton, accompanied the signing of the first part of what became known as the Oslo accords. That first agreement, the Declaration of Principles (DOP), outlined a new relationship between the two sides, following more than a year of secret negotiations held in the Norwegian capital and under the auspices of its government.

The agreement signed September 13, 1993, between the PLO and Israel did not bring an independent Palestinian state into being; it did not call for an end to Israeli occupation or even use the word occupation. But it did transform the terrain on which the diplomatic and political efforts to end the conflict would be waged.

For the Palestinians, the DOP brought about two important goals. First was recognition of the PLO as the representative of the Palestinian people. Although discussions today usually focus on the PLO's weakness, the importance of this recognition should not be forgotten: It meant the reversal of a longstanding Israeli policy that rejected the PLO because it represented the Palestinians as a separate people, inside and outside the occupied territories; therefore, it meant that Israel recognized that the solution to the conflict could not be limited only to those Palestinians living under occupation in the West Bank and Gaza. Second, it called for redeployment of Israeli troops out of the Palestinian cities and population centers. It was not an end to military occupation, or even a withdrawal of troops (the troops remained throughout the occupied territories, on the roads, surrounding towns and villages, etc.). But for a while, until the re-occupations of 2002, it represented a major security improvement in the lives of ordinary Palestinians, who could now go to work or send their children to school without worrying about Israeli soldiers camped on their roofs or in the road in front of their houses. The DOP, however, did not include Israeli recognition of the Palestinian right to an independent state.

For the Israelis, the DOP brought official recognition by the Palestinians of Israel's right to exist, and a renunciation of terrorism and armed struggle. It opened the door to an end to the Arab boycott and the beginning of normalization of Israel's relations with Arab neighbors. That meant the opening of trade relations with surrounding countries, a potentially huge boon for Israel's high-tech advanced economy. It also allowed Israel to renege on its responsibility for the economic and social needs of the Palestinian population and for security for Israelis—all without ending actual Israeli control over the occupied territories.

### What was the Oslo process? How did the Oslo process start?

The Oslo process began while the official, public negotiations that followed the 1991 US-sponsored Madrid peace conference were still going on. But after ten sessions, those talks had stalled again in the spring of 1993, this time over the status of Jerusalem, and it was becoming clear they weren't going anywhere. Madrid's failure increased interest among the highest-level officials on both sides in the still-secret talks already underway in Oslo.

Those talks, initially involving Israeli academics and mid-level Palestinian officials brought together by Norway's foreign minister, had gone much further than the Madrid talks. They culminated in September 1993 with announcements that the parties had agreed to letters of mutual recognition and a Declaration of Principles. The US quickly moved in to take over sponsorship of the process, and the White House signing ceremony finalized the agreement.

Oslo's DOP separated the various issues that divided Israelis and Palestinians into two types: easy and hard. The theory was that the "easy" issues—such things as release of prisoners, economic cooperation, construction of Palestinian sea and airports, security considerations, etc.—would be dealt with first, during a five-year interim period. Discussion of the "hard" or final status issues—including borders of a Palestinian state, settlements, the status of Jerusalem, and the rights of refugees—would not even begin until the third year, and their resolution would be delayed till the end of the interim period (which was eventually extended from five to seven years).

### Why didn't the Oslo process work?

The problem was, the supposedly "easy" interim issues proved to be too difficult, and most were never resolved. As a result, no one ever even got around to discussing the final status questions. And no one— meaning the US, which remained the sponsor of the diplomatic process—was prepared to weigh in on the side of the Palestinians in the hope of balancing the extraordinary disparity of power that characterized relations between the two sides.

The Oslo process began under a Labor government in Israel. In November 1995, Prime Minister

Yitzhak Rabin, who had signed the Oslo Declaration of Principles with Yasir Arafat two years earlier, was assassinated by an extremist Jewish Israeli. By May 1996, the right-wing Likud Bloc had won the new Israeli elections, defeating Rabin's Labor Party successor Shimon Peres, and bringing to power Benjamin Netanyahu as prime minister. Netanyahu had campaigned against the Oslo accords, and when elected he reneged on almost all of the Israeli troop redeployments his predecessor had agreed to. He continued the construction of settlements and bypass roads in the occupied territories that the Labor Party had in fact encouraged, and consolidated the most nationalistic settlers as a core component of his constituency.

When the Labor Party returned to power in 1999, another hard-line general, Ehud Barak, became prime minister. He escalated the pace of settlement-building even beyond that of Netanyahu, resisted troop redeployments, increased closures of Palestinian territory and house demolitions, and raised the government subsidies to settlements in the occupied territories.

For Palestinians, things went from bad to worse, and diplomatic exchanges between the two sides still trying to implement Oslo's "interim" issues dwindled. Economy, health, education, and security all deteriorated for ordinary Palestinians, and the hope that many Palestinians had placed in the Oslo process faded.

So in the summer of 2000, nearing the end of his presidency, having invested a huge amount of personal prestige in figuring out a solution to the conflict, Bill Clinton summoned the top Israeli and Palestinian leaders to Camp David for a summit to jump straight into the final status issues. It was a go-for-broke plan, in which negotiators would immediately face the central issues that had divided Israelis and Palestinians, and had brought about the failure of earlier diplomatic efforts, for years.

### What were Oslo's "final status" issues? Why were they so difficult?

The four key issues were: 1) the nature and borders of a Palestinian state; 2) the status of Jerusalem; 3) the right to return for Palestinian refugees; and 4) Israeli settlements in the occupied territories. They were the most difficult, individually and collectively, because they represent the fundamental issues of Israeli control and Palestinian national aspirations. Further, although they are all subject to international law and specific UN resolutions, Israel (backed by the US) rejects international jurisdiction and even the relevance of international law and international actors other than the United States.

### Whose capital is Jerusalem?

When the United Nations voted to partition Palestine in 1947, it identified land that was supposed to become an Israeli Jewish state, and land for a

Palestinian Arab state. It also imposed a special status—*corpus separatum*, or separate body—for Jerusalem, ordering that Jerusalem remain under international, that is UN, jurisdiction, separately from the two new states that were to be created. The UN recognized the international significance of Jerusalem, whose holy sites are central to the tenets of the three Abrahamic monotheistic religions (Islam, Christianity, and Judaism), and viewed international jurisdiction as the best way to ensure both protection of the holy sites and free access to all.

When the 1947–48 conflict ended, Israel controlled 78 percent of the territory of Palestine, but only the western half of Jerusalem, comprising largely the "new" city, and excluding both the Old City and the overwhelmingly Arab East Jerusalem. Israel promptly announced that Jerusalem would be its capital. East Jerusalem, like the rest of the Palestinian West Bank, came under Jordanian administration.

In 1967, when Israel occupied the last 22 percent of the territory, including East Jerusalem, it immediately annexed East Jerusalem, and declared the "unification" of the city. Israel immediately began construction of huge settlement blocs in Arab East Jerusalem, and today more than 200,000 Israeli Jews live in East Jerusalem. But no country in the world officially recognizes Jerusalem as the capital of Israel. All other embassies, including that of the US, are located in Tel Aviv.

The US Congress has routinely voted to recognize Jerusalem as the official capital of Israel and to move the US embassy to Jerusalem, and US presidents have routinely campaigned for office on such commitments. But no president has taken that step, recognizing such a move as a threat to regional stability. When Congress passed legislation requiring the relocation of the US embassy to Jerusalem, both the Clinton and George W. Bush administrations made use of the six-month waiver clause in order to keep the status quo.

Palestinians have long claimed Jerusalem as the capital of their would-be state. Their proposal is based on the idea of "one city, two capitals," in which the city would remain undivided, but there would be two national capitals within it—Israel's capital in West Jerusalem, Palestine's capital in East Jerusalem. The models of Italy and the Vatican, who both have capitals in Rome, as well as other historical examples, are often invoked.

During the Oslo process, particularly in the Camp David summit of August 2000, the Israelis rejected the Palestinian proposal. Their offer was based on maintaining full Israeli sovereignty over all of Jerusalem. The Palestinians were offered a kind of municipal autonomy in Arab neighborhoods of East Jerusalem (excluding the Jewish settlements in East Jerusalem), including the right to fly a Palestinian flag from the mosques of the Haram al-Sharif (known to Jews as the Temple Mount) in Jerusalem's Old City.

Israel would also extend the municipal border of Jerusalem to encompass three small Palestinian villages east of the city. Israel would then allow the Palestinians to change the name of one of those towns, Abu Dis, to al-Quds (the Arabic name for Jerusalem), and it would become the capital of Palestine. The problem, of course, was that changing the name of a tiny, dusty village to al-Quds would not transform it into the city of Jerusalem—and calling it "the capital" wouldn't make it so.

International law governing the illegality of holding territory obtained through war, and a host of UN resolutions specifically calling for an end to Israel's occupation of East Jerusalem, require the creation of a Palestinian capital in Arab East Jerusalem. Israel's insistence on maintaining full sovereignty over the occupied Arab sector of the city violates those international decisions, particularly after the municipal borders of "Greater Jerusalem" were expanded from 4 square miles in 1967 to about 47 square miles at the expense of more than 20 Palestinian villages in the West Bank, which then came under Israeli control.

### What happened to Israeli settlements and settlers during the years of the Oslo process?

Construction of new settlements and expansion of existing settlements in the occupied territories were already increasing by the time the Oslo process began in 1993. The settler population was growing by about

10 percent a year, even during the Labor Party government of the late Yitzhak Rabin. In fact, the years that Rabin's government was in power saw the largest expansion of the settlements since they began in 1968.

In 1998, Israel began construction on a new settlement named Har Homa, on a West Bank hillside known as Jabal Abu-Ghneim lying between Jerusalem and Beit Sahour. It caused enormous opposition because it was the final link in a ring of settlements surrounding East Jerusalem that together served to cut off access from Arab East Jerusalem to the West Bank. It led to new UN debates about the settlements as a violation of the Geneva Conventions. But the protests led nowhere, building continued, and by mid-2002 Israeli Jewish residents were filling the gleaming white stone, ultra-modern settlement apartments.

From the beginning of Oslo until 2002, the settler population almost doubled. While the US-backed road map of 2003 called for a freeze in settlement construction as a "confidence-building measure" by Israel, the expansion continued. Currently the Israeli settler population in the occupied territories has topped 440,000—about 240,000 in the West Bank, 200,000 in Arab East Jerusalem. In less than three years, from 2004 to September 2006, Israel had put on the market 3,207 new homes in West Bank settlements, anticipating an expansion of the settler population—prohibited under the terms of the road map—by 16,000–20,000 additional settlers.

The continued existence and expansion of the settlements remains an enormous obstacle in to peace. They all—whether authorized by the Israeli government or not—violate the Geneva Conventions, which specifically prohibit the transfer of anyone from the occupying country to the occupied territory. Further, the settlements, and the settlers-only or "bypass" roads that connect them and link them to cities inside Israel, and especially the Apartheid Wall built on West Bank land, all serve to divide the territories into separate cantons surrounded by Israeli troops, and prevent the creation of a contiguous Palestinian state. These roads, and much of the settler infrastructure, mostly built during the Oslo period, have been constructed on confiscated Palestinian land, and funded with United States tax money.

### What would a Palestinian "state" as determined by Oslo/Camp David have looked like?

In October 1995, Israeli Prime Minister Yitzhak Rabin declared Israel would not return to the 1967 borders as required under international law. He said Jerusalem would remain unified and under exclusive Israeli sovereignty, and that most of the settlements would remain. Further, he described the Palestinian "entity" to be created as something "less than a state."

What Israel proposed at Camp David in August 2000 (the first occasion when final status issues were directly negotiated) was a Palestinian "state" in something approaching 80 percent of the West Bank plus Gaza. The capital would not be in Jerusalem, although some limited municipal authority in Palestinian neighborhoods might be granted. The 20 percent of the West Bank that Israel would keep would be made up of the settlements, military bases, and, crucially, the bypass roads that effectively divide the West Bank into separate regions. It was as though a family's house had been occupied against their will for many years, and they were suddenly told that they could have all the rooms back, but the occupier was going to keep control of the hallways between the rooms. How much of a home would that be?

Israel proposed maintaining control of two major east–west highways, which would cut the West Bank into three completely separate, non-contiguous areas. Key water sources, underground aquifers, would remain under Israeli control, as would external borders and air space. About 20 percent of the West Bank settlers, primarily from small isolated settlements, would be resettled inside Israel; the other 80 percent, including the large settlement blocs, would remain under Israeli jurisdiction and under the protection of the Israeli army; the Palestinian state would have no authority over the settlers. Newer versions of this Sharon plan, agreed to by Sharon and Bush in the April 2004 letter exchange and later known as the "convergence" plan of Sharon's successor, Ehud Olmert, remained official Israeli policy until the summer 2006 war in Gaza and Lebanon changed the political equation.

# OSLO AGREEMENT

0      20 km

Jenin
GANIM

Tulkarem

SHAVEI
SHOMRON

Nablus
ELON MOREH

Qalqilya

ALFEI
MENASHE

ARIEL

MA'ALE
EPHRAIM

RIMONIM

PSAGOT
Ramallah

GIV'AT
ZE'EV

Jericho

Jerusalem
MA'ALE
ADUMIM

ISRAEL
KALYA

Bethlehem

ETZION
BLOC

Green Line

Dead Sea

KIRYAT ARBA

Hebron

| | |
|---|---|
| ▨ | Area A - Palestinian cities |
| ▨ | Area B - Palestinian villages |
| ▨ | Area C - Israeli settlement, military areas and state lands |
| ▲ | Main Israeli settlements |

## *What happened at Camp David? Why did it fail?*

The Camp David summit reflected an almost desperate effort by President Clinton to salvage the failing Oslo peace process before the end of his second term. Although the origins of Oslo were not in a US diplomatic effort, Washington had taken on sponsorship of the peace process, and the September 1993 Rabin—Arafat photo opportunity remained the high point of Clinton's presidency. There is little question that by 2000 the president was eager for a new photo-op to burnish his scandal-tarnished place in history. Ehud Barak, Israel's then prime minister, whose lackluster term was also coming to an end, persuaded Clinton to convene the ill-prepared summit.

Camp David reflected the failure of Oslo's seven-year-long "peace process." Palestinian lives had deteriorated, unemployment was up, incomes were down, and the euphoria that had greeted the White House handshake seven years earlier had turned into bitter resentment and rising anger. Until Camp David, Israeli and Palestinian negotiators had never even opened talks on the difficult final status issues. Clinton's view was that by leapfrogging over the "interim" issues and going straight to the fundamentals—state and borders, settlements, Jerusalem, and refugees—it might be possible to rescue the process and, in the process, his legacy.

But that would have been possible only if the US was prepared to demand serious concessions from

Israel, its longstanding ally and the holder of all the cards. Instead the Clinton administration acted as though the talks were between two equal partners who bore equal power and responsibility to make compromises and concessions instead of between an occupying power and an occupied population. In fact, the problem at Camp David was precisely that the disparity of power that had long characterized Israeli–Palestinian negotiations remained unchallenged; President Clinton did nothing to try to balance the thoroughly lopsided playing field. The talks persisted for two weeks, through sleepless nights and intensive days, through Bill Clinton's hasty departure for the G-8 summit in Okinawa and his hurried return. The official post-summit statement issued jointly by the Palestinian, Israeli, and American sides called the talks "unprecedented in both scope and detail." But in the end they failed anyway.

### Didn't Israeli Prime Minister Ehud Barak make the most generous offer in history to the Palestinians? Why did they reject it?

President Clinton, understanding the difficulties and potential pitfalls that lay ahead, had promised both parties that he would not blame either side if the talks collapsed. But when the talks broke down he pointed his finger squarely at Yasir Arafat and the Palestinians. Perhaps the most widely repeated claim after Camp David was that of Barak's "generous offer" to the Palestinians. It was, we were told over and over again, the most generous offer any Israeli official had ever made.

That statement, technically, was absolutely true. It was also, however, absolutely irrelevant. The standard against which any serious diplomatic offer made by a country illegally occupying another must be judged is not how well it compares to earlier offers made by that same occupying power; it must be judged against the requirements of international law. And from that standard, Barak's offer was far from generous. The "generous offer" was a myth.

More important than the offer's generosity compared to earlier Israeli offers was the fact that, according to Clinton negotiator Robert Malley, it was simply not true that "Israel's offer met most if not all of the Palestinians' legitimate aspirations." That was the reason Palestinians rejected the offer. One can certainly question the wisdom of a diplomatic strategy that did not provide an immediate counter-proposal to an unacceptable offer. But there should be little difficulty in understanding why Palestinian negotiators would reject an offer based on a set of disconnected pieces of territory amounting to only 80 percent of the remaining 22 percent of historic Palestine; a network of roads, bridges and tunnels accessible only to Israeli settlers and permanently guarded by Israeli soldiers; permanent loss of water resources; no shared sovereignty in Jerusalem; the right of return for refugees not even up for discussion; and with 80 percent of the illegal settlers to remain in place.

## What would a real, comprehensive peace have looked like at Camp David?

A comprehensive peace would have called for an end to Israeli occupation—all the occupation, withdrawing Israeli troops from all of the West Bank and Gaza, returning Israel's borders to those of June 4, 1967. It would have called for an independent Palestinian state in the entire West Bank and Gaza Strip, with the Palestinian capital in East Jerusalem, and the entire city of Jerusalem open between the two countries. It would have announced the closure of all settlements as Israeli military enclaves, with settlers given the option of moving back to Israel with compensation, or remaining in their settlement towns as ordinary citizens of the new Palestinian state. It would have acknowledged the Palestinian right of return and opened negotiations on how to implement that right. It would have created security guarantees for both the Israeli and Palestinian peoples, perhaps including international assistance in monitoring borders. As called for in the 2002 Saudi/Arab League peace proposal, normalization of relations between Israel and all the Arab countries would follow the end of Israel's occupation.

Then, the hard work of rebuilding a shattered economy and shattered society in Palestine, and rebuilding shattered lives in both Palestine and Israel, could begin.

# PART IV

LOOKING BACKWARD (1900–1991)

### What was the Madrid peace conference in 1991?

When the Gulf War ended in 1991 with the defeat of Iraq and the US triumphant and unchallenged across the Middle East, Washington turned toward redrawing the political map of the region. The goal reflected a continuation of the US rationale for the war itself: Iraq's illegal invasion of Kuwait had provided a convenient pretext for the US to lead the world to war, to prove it remained a superpower even as the Cold War ended. Now it would prove it could orchestrate a regional peace the same way. And it would do so at a moment of terrible division in the Arab world, division rooted in Iraq's invasion of a fellow Arab country. Palestinian leaders had opposed the US war build-up, as did public opinion in the Arab world, and supported earlier attempts to bring about a joint Arab solution, but together with Jordan, they refrained from supporting the US war effort; one result was the erosion of long-standing Arab government support for Palestinian national rights, the expulsion of thousands of Palestinians from Saudi Arabia and other Gulf states, and the significant weakening of the Palestinian diplomatic position in the Arab world and beyond.

The Madrid peace conference was ostensibly under joint US-Soviet invitation, but with the Soviet Union about to collapse, there was no question that Washington was in sole charge. Madrid was designed to look like the long-sought international peace conference—invitations were sent to the European Union, Japan, many Arab countries, and more—but the glittering international gala provided only the ceremonial opening to the actual negotiations. And those were—as Israel had long demanded—in the form of separate bilateral talks between Israel and each of its Arab interlocutors, Syria, Lebanon, and Jordan.

It was only within the confines of the Israel–Jordan talks that the Palestinians were even included; they were denied the right to participate as a separate delegation and were only a sub-set of the Jordanian team. Israel also had won US agreement to accept Israel's severe restrictions on who could negotiate on behalf of the Palestinians.

Madrid was very much an American initiative. President George H. W. Bush, opening the conference, said its aim was to achieve a "just, lasting, and comprehensive peace" in the Middle East, not simply to end the state of war and replace it with a state of non-belligerency. Bush identified his goals as peace treaties, security, trade, economic relations, investment, "even tourism." Significantly, he did not speak of justice, ending occupation, or Palestinian independence as goals to be fought for or protected in the context of the Madrid talks.

Bush's plan called for five years of Palestinian "self-government," in the third year of which negotiations would begin for a final resolution of the status of the occupied territories—very close to the Oslo formula that would later replace the Madrid process. He claimed that this "self-government" would "give the Palestinian people meaningful control of their own lives," while "taking into account Israeli security." Bush appropriated Israel's own formula, describing how Palestinians under "self-rule" would be allowed to control their own lives, but there was no change in maintaining Israel's control of the land. Soviet President Mikhail Gorbachev focused primarily on the international context for the peace conference, and described Middle East peace in words that evoked Dr. Martin Luther King—defining peace as "not merely the cessation of war, but of moving towards justice." His country, however, would disappear from the map less than two months later, and his words had little relevance.

### What kind of diplomacy followed the Madrid conference?

After the ceremonies in Madrid, the diplomats got down to work in bilateral talks based in Washington. A parallel set of multilateral talks on issues such as refugees, water, and economic development brought together much broader governmental participation, including Canada, Japan, and the European Union, first in an opening conference in Moscow in January 1992, and followed by separate meetings in the scattered capitals.

The various sets of talks plodded along in fits and starts for the next eighteen months or so. Little progress was made on the Israeli—Palestinian front, and frustrations grew higher. The impasse involved two principal issues: Israel's refusal to come to terms with its role as occupier, and to make any commitment to stop building the illegal settlements.

As months passed, and Palestinian and Israeli diplomats returned to State Department conference rooms for round after round of fruitless diplomacy, a growing realization emerged that Madrid was failing. The PLO faced the task of simultaneously orchestrating the officially non-PLO diplomatic team in the Madrid process while trying to provide international grounding to the continuing intifada going on at home. Developments were getting dire, and it was in that period of Madrid's stalemate that the secret back-channel Oslo talks began.

The urgency of the PLO may also have been rooted in the organization's growing understanding of the US role. Round ten of the Madrid talks collapsed over the issue of Jerusalem. Prior to that round, some hope had lingered among at least some of the Palestinian diplomats that the Clinton administration would stake out a position rooted in its claimed commitment to human rights—rather than in its well-known close ties to Israel. When Secretary of State Warren Christopher not only accepted the legitimacy of Israel's position (that occupied Arab East Jerusalem be excluded from the interim Palestinian authority) but also demanded that the Palestinians sign a "joint statement of principles" based on that position, the Palestinians realized they could not hope for an even-handed sponsor in Washington, and the talks collapsed. The loss of that hoped-for US role, and the resulting recognition that Madrid was a failure, may have set the stage for a new level of Palestinian urgency in the Oslo talks.

## What happened to Israel and Palestine during the 1991 Gulf War?

Iraq's invasion of Kuwait opened a huge rift in an Arab world once unified, at least rhetorically, in support of Palestinian rights. Viewed as siding with Iraq, the Palestinians were quickly ostracized by many Arab leaders, particularly in the wealthy Gulf states. The rift grew as more Arab states agreed or succumbed to pressure to join the US-led coalition. Palestinian abandonment grew more severe.

In Israel, the threat of attack by Iraq grew. Rumors of Iraqi chemical or biological weapons fed the fears among Israelis; gas masks were distributed and citizens were instructed to create sealed rooms in their homes to protect them from chemicals. Palestinians living under Israeli occupation were largely denied gas masks, engendering fury across the occupied territories, to the degree that some Palestinians actually cheered the prospect of incoming Scud missiles. In order to maintain Arab participation in the coalition, the US demanded that Israel not retaliate even to a direct Iraqi strike. In return, the US agreed to protect Israel.

When fighting began, Iraq did indeed fire several dozen missiles on Israeli cities. None were armed with chemical or biological weapons, and none did major damage. Casualties included two Israelis killed in the attacks, along with some who died from stress-related heart attacks and from misuse of gas masks. Israel did not respond militarily to the Iraqi strikes.

The end of the war, with Iraq qualitatively defeated and weakened, left Israel in a very strong position. It used its elevated influence in Washington to shape the terms of the post-war Madrid conference—including functional exclusion of the United Nations, and severe restrictions on the nature of Palestinian participation. Those restrictions included rejection of a separate Palestinian delegation, and Israel's right to veto all Palestinian participants to ensure that only Palestinians from the West Bank and Gaza could negotiate for the Palestinians. Any Palestinians from East Jerusalem, anyone with official ties to the PLO, and anyone from the far-flung Palestinian diaspora were excluded by Israeli fiat.

The major compromise the Palestinians had made in 1988, when they declared an independent state and accepted a two-state solution—thus accepting a state on only 22 percent of their historic territory—was largely ignored after the Gulf War. The intifada that began in 1987 had brought new credibility and political power to the Palestinians and the PLO; by the end of the Gulf crisis, most of that momentary power was lost.

### What was the first "intifada" all about?

In the twenty years after Israel first took over the West Bank and Gaza in 1967, a new generation, half the population, grew up knowing nothing but military occupation. Unlike their parents, many of whom still dreamed of returning to their homes inside Israel (a dream that would later be reclaimed by the third generation of refugees and exiles), these teenagers and young adults built their future hopes around creation of a Palestinian state in the West Bank, Gaza, and East Jerusalem.

Repression, despair, and, for some, passivity all grew. Then, on December 8, 1987, near the densely crowded checkpoint at the entrance to the Gaza Strip, an Israeli truck swerved and struck and killed four Palestinians: a doctor, an engineer, and two laborers. Some said it was deliberate, though no one knew for sure. What made the incident extraordinary was the outcome. Palestinian outrage sparked an uprising that swept across the Gaza Strip, spread to the West Bank, and set into motion a blaze of nationalist resistance to occupation.

The uprising soon came to be called the "intifada," a word whose Arabic roots refer to rising up, or shaking off. It began as spontaneous actions, stone-throwing children and young people challenging the troops and tanks of Israel's occupying army. But soon it became more organized, as existing grassroots organizations, most of them linked to various factions of the PLO, mobilized to respond to new conditions, and to answer the needs of the population in the context of Israel's increasingly repressive response.

Women's, worker's, medical, student's, agri-cultural, and community organizations took on new tasks—growing food in home and community gardens to replace the Israeli goods now being boycotted;

guarding village streets at night with whistles to warn of soldiers on their way; maintaining mobile clinics to provide emergency medical help to villages or towns under curfew; boycotting taxes. A daily commercial strike was soon declared that shut down Palestinian businesses at noon in a sign of unity and resistance. What came to be called the UNLU—Unified National Leadership of the Uprising—emerged clandestinely, distributing leaflets overnight that provided information about coming strike days, special commemorations of the intifada, or particular constituencies to be mobilized at particular times.

But throughout, there was a unified view that only the PLO, with its leadership in exile in Tunis, could speak for the Palestinians. Every international envoy who showed up in East Jerusalem or Ramallah or Gaza City was told the same thing: our address is in Tunis. If you want to engage us diplomatically, talk to the PLO. The UNLU itself included representatives of all the major PLO factions.

While there were some diplomatic gains, by far the major advance of the intifada was visible internally, within Palestinian society itself. The opening up of new ideas, new empowerment of women and young people, new levels of community involvement and participation, all would last beyond the intifada itself.

It was only with the exaggerated enthusiasm that greeted the signing of Oslo's Declaration of Principles, in September 1993, that the first intifada began to wind down. For the next seven years, Oslo, rather than intifada, would be the code word on everyone's tongue.

### What were conditions like in the occupied territories before the first intifada?

In some ways it was surprising that the uprising did not erupt earlier. Conditions were dire, jobs few, money scarce. Education was central to Palestinian families, and many young university graduates headed abroad for professional training or to find work as doctors, engineers, and more. For most families, particularly the half of the population who lived in the refugee camps, it was a daily struggle to meet the most basic needs.

Israel's military presence was everywhere, although the closures and curfews that became commonplace later were rare. The PLO was outlawed, and expressions of support for it could land one in prison. Arrests, indefinite detention, and even expulsions were common. Israel tried to create a compliant leadership to compete with the PLO; nationalist political figures, such as the popularly elected local mayors, were targeted by Israelis. In one incident three mayors were attacked, killing one and leaving two badly maimed. There was an international consensus on ending the occupation and creating a Palestinian state, but there seemed to be no way to implement that view. The UN was unable to enforce its resolutions because the US protected Israel's occupation. Arab governments talked of liberating

Jerusalem and supporting Palestinian rights, but it remained all talk. International law seemed irrelevant.

### How did Israel come to be in control of the West Bank, Gaza, and East Jerusalem?

The 1967 Six-Day War began with Israel's attack on the Egyptian air force, which was wiped out within a few hours. Some argue that Israel's first strike was justified because Egypt, Syria, and Jordan were massing armies near Israel's borders. Certainly the tensions on all sides were on the rise. Egypt's nationalist president, Gamal Abdul Nasser, had demanded that the UN withdraw the emergency forces stationed on Egyptian territory since the 1956 Anglo-French-Israeli attack on Egypt. Although Israel had refused to grant the UN the right to station forces on its side of the border in 1956, it considered the withdrawal as a justification to go to war against Egypt.

But war still might have been prevented; just before Israel struck, Nasser had agreed to send his vice president to Washington for negotiations. Israel's attack was at least partly to prevent Nasser from using his Washington trip as a face-saving way to pull back his forces; such a move would have undermined what Israel saw as justification for its own attack. Israeli and US military officials agreed that the war had been Israel's decision. Israel's right-wing Likud bloc leader and later Prime Minister Menachem Begin told the Pentagon's Army War College in 1982 that "in June 1967 we again had a choice. The Egyptian Army concentrations in the Sinai approaches do not prove that Nasser was really about to attack us. We must be honest with ourselves. We decided to attack him."

Whatever one thinks about the legitimacy of Israel's war, it is clear that although it was aimed at the Arab states surrounding Israel, it was the Palestinians who paid the highest price. Even after the ceasefire, Israeli troops moved into Syria and captured the Golan Heights; 90,000 Golani Syrian Arabs were expelled. By the end of the war, Israel occupied Syria's Golan Heights, the Egyptian Sinai Peninsula, and the Palestinian West Bank and Gaza Strip. Two hundred fifty thousand more Palestinians were forced into exile, and over a million more were now under Israeli military occupation.

### What was the international community's response to the 1967 war?

The 1967 war provided the United Nations with its first opportunity to articulate a clear position on the once-accepted practice of victorious nations simply keeping, as colonies or expansions of existing territorial control, the nations it conquered and occupied. This practice was finally deemed unacceptable, and Security Council Resolution 242, on which most future Israel—Palestine negotiations would be based, asserted "the inadmissibility of the acquisition of territory by war." It was an unequivocal position.

Other parts of the resolution were less precise. While almost every nation agreed that Israel should return all of the captured territories it was occupying, there was some diplomatic wrangling with the US. The final result was a dodge: the French version called for the return of "the territories," implying all the land that Israel held; the English version spoke of returning "territories," leaving open the possibility that partial return might be acceptable. From that moment, Israel adopted the position that it was not obligated to return all the territories. With its return of the Sinai Peninsula to Egypt after the Camp David Accords of 1979 between Israel and Egypt, Israel claimed that since the virtually unpopulated Sinai desert represented the largest percentage of land it had occupied in 1967, its return to Egypt should be sufficient to meet the UN's demand. Any further return of occupied land, to Palestinians or Syria, would be at Israel's choice and on Israel's terms.

From 1967 until today, the UN has passed numerous resolutions calling for an end to Israel's occupation, but those resolutions remain unfulfilled.

### How did the US respond to the occupation?

At the time of the Six-Day War, US relations with Israel were friendly and supportive, but not anything close to the "special relationship" that has defined US–Israeli ties since that time. In 1967, the Pentagon predicted that the balance of forces was so one-sided that no matter who struck first, no combination of Arab forces would overcome Israel's superior strength. But nonetheless, on May 25 the Pentagon sent battalions of Marines to the Sixth Fleet, then cruising the Mediterranean, in case they were needed to bolster Israel. By June 2, the date was set for Israel to teach Syria and Egypt the long-awaited "lesson." But first Israel needed permission from the US. On June 4, even as Nasser was negotiating with the US representative in Cairo, President Lyndon Johnson telegraphed Defense Minister Moshe Dayan and gave Israel the final green light. The next day, Dayan ordered the attack.

After the war, relations between the US and Israel became much closer. In the US, the war was presented as evidence of a heroic Israeli David triumphing over the aggressive Arab Goliath. Support skyrocketed for closer US ties to Israel. Fundraising by Zionist organizations, blood drives, and volunteer campaigns all soared. During the six days of the war, the United Jewish Appeal sold $220 million worth of Israeli bonds; American contributions for Israel in 1967 totalled $600 million.

But the biggest gain was not those individual contributions. Even more important was the new recognition in Washington of Israel's usefulness. It was the middle of the Cold War, after all, and Israel's military prowess showed US policymakers how valuable an ally it could be as the regional policeman for US oil and security interests in the Middle East. Soon Israel's junior partner role would be expanded to include Cold War battlefields much farther afield— such places as Angola, Mozambique, El Salvador, Chile,

Guatemala —where Israeli military assistance, training, and arms bolstered unsavory US allies.

Just ten days after the Six-Day War ended, a State Department memo noted "Israel has probably done more for the US in the Middle East in relation to money and effort invested than any of our so-called allies and friends elsewhere around the world since the end of the Second World War. In the Far East, we can get almost nobody to help us in Vietnam. Here, the Israelis won the war singlehandedly, have taken us off the hook, and have served our interests as well as theirs."

The reward, for Israel, was a flood of sophisticated weapons, including advanced Phantom jets. In the four years after the 1967 war, Israel would receive $1.5 billion in US arms—ten times as much as the total for the twenty years previous.

Given all of that, Israel's occupation of Palestinian land was hardly a concern for Washington. Over the years, different US presidents criticized the settlements in the occupied territories, variously describing them as "unhelpful," "obstacles to peace," or, briefly, "illegal." But little action matched the words. America's presumed strategic interests seemed to outweigh humanitarian and legal concerns in the Middle East.

### What was the 1982 Lebanon war all about? What was Ariel Sharon's role?

In 1970, after a bitter battle with the Jordanian military, the PLO moved its headquarters from

Jordan to Lebanon. Hundreds of thousands of Palestinian civilians followed, and the existing camps in Lebanon were soon crowded with refugees. Lebanon was soon a key focal point in the Israeli—Palestinian conflict.

With hundreds of thousands of Palestinian refugees living in Beirut and southern Lebanon, much of the governing, from schools and hospitals to licensing and legal systems, was taken over by the PLO. From 1975, Lebanon was stuck in a bloody civil war, pitting sectarian and religious factions against each other. Palestinian guerrillas and Israeli troops also continued to trade rocket fire across the Israeli—Lebanese border. In 1978, Israel invaded and took over a strip of southern Lebanon, and continued to occupy it in defiance of UN Resolution 425, which called for Israel to immediately and unconditionally withdraw. Instead, Israel sponsored an anti-Palestinian Christian-led militia called the South Lebanon Army, arming, paying, training, and supporting them in the occupied zone.

Israel's real goal was to destroy the PLO infrastructure—social as well as military—in Lebanon, and to put in place a compliant, pro-Israeli regime in Beirut. In 1982, when it appeared that Lebanon's civil war could drag on forever without those goals being achieved, Israel decided to move on its own. But first it needed to be sure its allies in Washington would approve.

Ensuring US support was a little bit tricky. After all, the US-brokered ceasefire between Israel and the

PLO in south Lebanon and across Israel's northern border had held for almost a year. There wasn't an obvious provocation on which to claim that a direct Israeli invasion was "necessary for self-defense." In May 1982, Israeli Defense Minister Ariel Sharon went to Washington to meet with President Reagan's secretary of state, Alexander Haig. Former President Jimmy Carter said after a national security briefing that "the word I got from very knowledgeable people in Israel is that 'we have a green light from Washington.'"

Once US backing was assured, a new provocation was created. On June 3, a renegade, anti-PLO Palestinian faction attempted to assassinate Israel's ambassador in London. The British police immediately identified Abu Nidal's forces as responsible, and revealed that PLO leaders themselves were among those on the would-be assassins' hit list. The PLO had nothing to do with the London attack. But Israel claimed the attack (the ambassador remained unhurt) was a justification for war against the PLO. Three days later, on June 6, 1982, the Israeli army invaded Lebanon in Operation "Peace for Galilee," crossing the Litani River and moving almost as far north as Beirut, destroying the feeble resistance from local villagers and from the United Nations peacekeeping troops swept aside in the assault. Israel remained in virtually uncontested control of the air, and had overwhelming military superiority on land and sea. Beirut was besieged and subjected to merciless bombing for two months. Casualties were enormous, totaling more than 17,000 Lebanese and Palestinians, mostly civilians. Hospitals were hit, and the Palestinian refugee camps were leveled in massive bombardment. General Ariel Sharon, then minister of defense and later prime minister of Israel, was at the center of planning and execution of the Lebanon invasion.

Israel relied overwhelmingly on US-supplied planes, bombs, and other military equipment in the offensive. But despite existing laws mandating that US military supplies be used only for defensive purposes, no one in Washington complained. The *New York Times* said, "American weapons were justly used to break the PLO." The Reagan administration and Congress both tried to outdo the other in calls to raise US aid to Israel. Throughout June and July the siege of Beirut continued, with inhabitants in the city in constant danger and many deprived of adequate food, water, and electricity. The bombing intensified in early August, culminating on August 12 with eleven solid hours of bombing in one day. Condemnation poured in from around the world, and even the US issued a mild criticism. A ceasefire was eventually achieved.

The US brokered the terms of the ceasefire, which centered on the PLO leaving Beirut: its guerrillas, its doctors, its civilian infrastructure, its officials, everyone and everything would board ship heading for Tunis, almost as far from Palestine as one could get and still be in the Arab world. The US agreed to serve as guarantor of Israel's promises and as protector of the Palestinian civilians, primarily women, children, and old men, left behind. US Marines were deployed as the centerpiece of an international force with a 30-day mandate to guard Beirut during the withdrawal of the PLO fighters.

### What was the Sabra-Shatila massacre in Lebanon?

On September 1, 1982, President Reagan announced a new peace initiative between Israel and the Palestinians, which included a freeze on new settlements, limited autonomy for Palestinians in the West Bank and Gaza, and some version of a "Jordanian solution," plus lots of new economic and military aid for Israel. But Israel rejected the Reagan plan, and the initiative remained stalled; in the West Bank, Israel immediately launched several new settlements. At the same time, Israel was having unanticipated difficulties with the new president of Lebanon, Bashir Gemayel. Israel had expected Gemayel to be "their man" in Beirut, but unexpectedly he was emerging as a Lebanese nationalist instead.

On September 11, two weeks before the end of their official mandate, the last US Marines were withdrawn from Beirut. Three days later, Gemayel was assassinated. Within hours, Israel responded by invading the Muslim- (and formerly Palestinian-) dominated West Beirut. The invasion completely violated the guarantees of protection the US had negotiated with the PLO. After a few hours, Defense Minister Sharon announced that the Christian Phalangists, the most anti-Palestinian of all the

Christian militias, would actually enter the Palestinian camps, rather than the Israelis themselves. The senior Israeli commander met with the top Phalangist leaders and told them, he said, "to act humanely, and not to harm women, children and old people."

On Thursday, September 16, Israeli troops lit flares to light the way for their Phalangist allies to enter the Sabra and Shatila refugee camps, on the outskirts of West Beirut. The massacre that followed, of unarmed children, women, and old men, went on for three days. It resulted in the deaths of between 2,000 and 3,000 Palestinians, most left piled up or hastily buried in mass graves. The Red Cross later said it would be impossible to know exactly how many died.

There was no question that the Israeli soldiers knew what was going on inside—it was visible even without their high-powered binoculars, and the sound of machine-gun fire continued throughout the days and nights. Finally, the US pushed Israel to withdraw the Phalangists. The *Los Angeles Times* reported that US Special Envoy Morris Draper told the Israeli officers that "you must stop the massacres. They are obscene. I have an officer in the camp counting the bodies.... They are killing children. You are in absolute control of the area and therefore responsible for that area."

Israel would remain occupying a large strip of south Lebanon until 2000, when the mounting deaths and injuries of young Israeli soldiers at the hands of Hezbollah resistance forces (an organization created after the 1982 invasion) brought about a political outcry inside Israel. The occupation was finally ended unilaterally, implementing most of the requirements of Resolution 425 twenty-two years after it was passed. But a small piece of land known as Sheba'a Farms remained contested, and the Lebanon–Israel border remained tense and militarized, leading to Israel's widely condemned Lebanon War of 2006.

### Did the Palestinians demand national rights and an independent state before the 1967 war?

Like most parts of the Arab world, national conscious-ness in Palestine grew in the context of demographic changes and shifts in colonial control. During the 400 years of Ottoman Turkish control, Palestine was an identifiable region within the larger empire, but linked closely with what was then known as Greater Syria. With World War I and the collapse of the Ottoman Empire, Palestine became part of the British Empire. But even before that, beginning in the 1880s, the increasing influx of European Jewish settlers brought about a new national identity—a distinctly Palestinian consciousness—among the Muslims and Christians who were the overwhelming majority of Palestinian society. There was widespread unease about, and sporadic organizing campaigns against, the influx of Zionist European settlers, who were viewed as a threat to indigenous land ownership. But nation-states did not yet exist in the Arab world.

In 1922, when the French and British divided up the Arab world they had taken over from the defeated

Ottoman empire, Palestine was demarcated with specific borders, and turned over to Great Britain to rule as a Mandate territory under the approval of the League of Nations. It was in that period that national rights and the demand for independence first emerged among Palestinians. As more European settlers arrived, and the British made contradictory promises to the Arabs on one side and the Zionist leaders on the other, conflict escalated. Palestinian Arabs challenged the right of the new occupants to their land, as well as challenging the legitimacy of the British overlords in protecting the immigrants; the Zionist settlers, similarly, saw the indigenous Arabs (they denied for decades that there was an identifiable Palestinian people) as an impediment to their full settlement of the land, and resisted the British efforts to restrict the numbers of immigrants allowed in to Palestine.

That conflict, and the armed clashes that accompanied it, eventually led to the British decision that Palestine was ungovernable, which led them to turn Mandate authority over to the new United Nations. When the UN voted to partition Palestine in 1947, opposition came from the Arab states, but the only survey taken of Palestinian opinion to determine what they themselves wanted was ignored in the international debate. The Palestinians were given no voice. For many years the popular sentiment among Palestinians was a desire to reverse partition—to create a democratic and secular state for all its citizens in all of Israel and Palestine together.

The period after the 1967 war, when Israel occupied the last remnants of Palestine, corresponded with the rise of the PLO as a popular guerrilla organization. (It had originally been created by Arab governments in 1964.) The initial strategic approach of the PLO was the call for Palestinian national rights in the context of a democratic secular state in all of historic (Mandate) Palestine. By the mid-1970s, debate was underway within the organization about recognizing Israel and shifting to a two-state approach. In January 1976, the PLO, with support from Egypt, Syria, Jordan, and the Soviet Union, introduced a resolution in the UN calling for a two-state solution. The US vetoed the resolution.

In 1988, at the height of the first intifada, the PLO's parliament-in-exile, the Palestine National Council, voted to accept a two-state strategy, while declaring Palestine an independent state.

### How was the PLO viewed in the Arab Middle East, the UN, and in the rest of the world?

When the PLO was created, it was viewed by the Arab governments largely as an instrument of their own interests. Only after the existing guerrilla organizations became the major components of the PLO and Yasir Arafat became its leader in 1968 did it take on significant credibility among Palestinians themselves. During the early 1970s, political campaigns among Palestinian communities in the occupied territories and among refugees and exiles scattered throughout the world led to virtually unanimous support for the PLO as the voice of the still-stateless Palestinians.

In 1974, the United Nations invited Yasir Arafat, leader of the PLO, to address the General Assembly. Arafat spoke of bearing both a gun and an olive branch, and pleaded with delegates, "do not let the olive branch fall from my hand." That same year, the Assembly identified November 29, anniversary of the day of the partition resolution years before, as an International Day of Solidarity with the Palestinian people. It also recognized the PLO as the "sole legitimate representative of the Palestinian people," and invited the PLO to become an official non-state "observer" at the UN, allowing it participation in all debates, and welcoming a Palestinian ambassador.

While the PLO soon won diplomatic recognition in capitals across the world, Arab leaders were less than pleased at its independent stance. In Jordan in particular, King Hussein saw the rise of the PLO as a threat to Jordan's traditional influence in the West Bank and East Jerusalem. In 1982, when Ariel Sharon launched his "Jordan is Palestine" campaign, the king's opposition was seen as less than enthusiastic. Only with the first intifada, when virtually unanimous Palestinian rejection of Jordan's role became undeniable, did the king finally sever his kingdom's links to Palestinian institutions. When the PLO declared Palestine independent in 1988, the new state, which still controlled no land of its own, quickly attained diplomatic relations with more governments than recognized Israel.

To the US, the PLO was a terrorist organization and Yasir Arafat an arch-terrorist. It was the same epithet used to condemn Nelson Mandela's African National Congress and a host of other national liberation movements. It was the same accusation, in fact, that the British had hurled at Menachem Begin and other Zionist military leaders in the pre-state period of Israeli history. In 1975, Henry Kissinger had promised Israel that the US would never recognize or negotiate with the PLO.

When the UN again invited Arafat to address the General Assembly in November 1988, just after the Palestinian Declaration of Independence, the US refused to issue a visa, despite its obligations as host country of the United Nations. The entire UN— diplomats, security guards, translators, secretariat staff—packed up and flew to Geneva for one day to hear the PLO chairman. In that speech, Arafat again rejected terrorism and recognized Israel; the goal was to open a dialogue with the US. In an internationally broadcast press conference Arafat read his speech; word came from Washington that it wasn't good enough. The press corps was recalled to the auditorium in Geneva's Palais des Nations, and the revised speech read out. In return, the US allowed a mid-level diplomat, then ambassador to Tunisia, to open talks with the PLO. But the talks languished, and were soon canceled.

Only with the Oslo process, when the Palestinians had accepted Washington's centrality in the peace talks, did the US accept the PLO as a full-fledged negotiating partner. During Bill Clinton's presidency, Yasir Arafat was one of the most frequent international visitors to the White House.

In the first two years of the George W. Bush administration, however, Arafat remained untouchable. President Bush refused even to speak with the Palestinian leader when their paths crossed at the United Nations, and by the spring of 2002 called explicitly for the replacement of the PLO chairman and President of the Palestinian Authority. When President Arafat died in 2004, the US position was one of barely suppressed enthusiasm that in a "post-Arafat era" the PLO would prove far more malleable to US and Israeli interests.

### What is Zionism? Do all Jews support Zionism?

Zionism is a political movement that calls for the creation of a specifically Jewish state. When the movement began in the late 1880s, anti-Semitism was a powerful and growing force in Russia and Europe. Most Jews at that time believed that the best way to stop anti-Semitism was either through some kind of assimilation, or through alliances with other political movements. But a small number of Jews believed that anti-Semitism was a permanent feature of national and world politics, and that the only way for Jews to be safe would be for them to leave their home countries and establish a Jewish state elsewhere.

Early Zionist leaders believed that a Jewish state could be established anywhere (Uganda, Argentina, and Turkey were all considered at different times); it was a thoroughly secular movement. But the founder of the modern Zionist movement, Theodore Herzl, recognized that linking Zionism to Palestine would gain wider support for the movement among Jews, including more religious elements in the Jewish community who had not been early supporters. Herzl also believed that a Jewish state could only be created with the support of a colonial sponsor, and he traveled the imperial capitals of the world seeking a patron.

Many Jews opposed Zionism. The ultra-orthodox Jews in Palestine believed that only God could deliver a state to the Jewish people, and that a human-based effort was against God's will. Many Jews facing anti-Semitic attacks rejected Zionism's call for them to leave their homelands, seeing that position as reflecting the same demand to "get out of our country" of the anti-Semites themselves.

The Zionist movement won strong support from the British when London took control of Palestine with the defeat of the Ottoman Empire. In 1917, the Balfour Declaration stated that "His Majesty's Government views with favour the establishment in Palestine of a national home for the Jewish people, ... it being clearly understood that nothing shall be done which may prejudice the civil and religious rights of existing non-Jewish communities in Palestine." In the stroke of a pen the vast majority of the population of Palestine was reduced to the "non-Jewish community."

Zionism gradually gained more adherents, though slowly. It was only in the 1930s and '40s, as German, Polish, and other European Jews frantically sought to escape Hitler and their first-choice countries of refuge, the US and Britain, denied them entry, that Zionism and the call to create a Jewish state in Palestine became a more popular view among Jews. After World War II, with desperate Holocaust survivors filling displaced persons camps across Europe, Zionism became the majority position.

The Zionist slogan was that Palestine was "a land without a people for a people without a land." Certainly the second part was true—the European Jews who had escaped or survived the Holocaust had lost everything—their homes, their families, their countries, their land. Turned away from the US because of anti-Semitism, and encouraged to go to Palestine instead, it was not surprising that thousands flocked to join Jewish communities there. But the first part of the slogan hid the reality—for Palestine was not a land without a people. Its indigenous people had been there all along.

With the creation of the State of Israel, the organizations of the Zionist movement such as the Jewish Agency became adjuncts of the state apparatus, focusing on recruiting and settling Jews from all over the world in Israel.

—PART V—

THE FUTURE

### What would a just and comprehensive peace between Israel and Palestine look like today?

Almost all Palestinians today are looking for a solution based on international law and UN resolutions, on human rights and equality for all. For most, that starts with the creation of a truly independent, sovereign, and democratic State of Palestine to be constructed on the 22 percent of historic Palestine that Israel occupied in 1967: the West Bank, Gaza Strip, and East Jerusalem. That means that all Israel troops would be withdrawn, and Israel's occupation would end. The State of Palestine would control entry and exit to and from its country, although the United Nations or other international monitors may be deployed on the borders around and between the two states to ensure their security.

Equality means both within and between states. Israel and Palestine, as equals, would jointly exchange full diplomatic relations. Israeli settlers would be disarmed and given the option of moving to new homes inside Israel, or remaining in their homes as citizens of Palestine with no special privileges and accountable to the Palestinian government. Jerusalem would be an open city, with two separate capitals within it: the capital of Israel in West Jerusalem, and the capital of Palestine in East Jerusalem.

A comprehensive peace would also include recognition of the right of Palestinian refugees to return to their homes. That starts with Israel's recognition of its role in the expulsion of refugees and creation of the refugee crisis in 1948, and public acceptance of Resolution 194 and the legal right of refugees to return, to which Israel agreed at the time it joined the United Nations in 1949. Once the right to return has been recognized, discussions about how best to implement it can begin.

Each state would be responsible for maintaining the safety and security of its own citizens, and would make commitments to prevent any cross-border attacks on civilians in the other's territory.

A comprehensive and lasting peace will also require economic arrangements that move quickly to reverse the humanitarian disaster currently prevailing among Palestinians, as well as addressing the vast disparity of economic power between the two countries. Technology transfer and job creation should be among the approaches considered.

Within each state, equality of all citizens would be guaranteed; there would be no privileges for Jews or discrimination against non-Jews in Israel, and none of the reverse in Palestine.

### Won't a Palestinian state be a threat to Israel's security? What about terrorism?

Israel is by far the strongest military power in the region; it is one of the strongest military powers in the world. Israel's nuclear capacity includes at least 200 high-density nuclear bombs, as well as a nuclear bomb production facility in the Negev desert at Dimona. Israel is not a signatory to the Nuclear Non-Proliferation Treaty (NPT), and refuses to allow international inspection of its nuclear arsenal as the treaty would require. Israel's military includes not only the newest and most advanced US-produced fighter-bombers, helicopter gunships, missile defense systems, and more, but relies on its own domestic production capacity as well, one of the most advanced arms-manufacturing systems in the world. Against such power, a new Palestinian state simply does not represent a serious threat to the national security of Israel. Many Palestinians look to Costa Rica, which voluntarily disarmed itself of an army, as a model for once Palestine's existence is secure.

The issue of the personal safety of individual Israelis is different. During the years of Israel's occupation of Palestine, resistance to that occupation has sometimes taken illegal forms, including attacks on civilians inside Israel. But the overwhelming majority of attacks on civilians—terrorist attacks—however illegal, were in fact waged in response to Israel's occupation; with the end of occupation, the overwhelming majority of attacks will end. Certainly both Israel and Palestine will have an obligation to protect their own citizens from cross-border (or internal) terrorist attacks. When a fully independent and sovereign Palestinian state can develop normal relations of equality with Israel, as opposed to the distorted relationship of occupied and occupier, it will be possible to cooperate on security issues as well.

## *How would a secure Israel and an independent Palestine living side by side affect the Middle East and the rest of the world?*

The conflict between Israel and the Palestinians has destabilized the entire Middle East region. Popular anger toward Israel because of the occupation and the human rights violations inherent to it is sky-high and rising. Arab governments, themselves facing serious crises of legitimacy, have to balance their people's rage against demands from the US to maintain stability and some level of normal relations with Israel. Because most Arab regimes are so dependent on the United States—either economically (Jordan), militarily (Saudi Arabia, Kuwait, Qatar), or both (Egypt)—they have little choice but to accede to Washington's wishes. But doing so further isolates them from their people, and raises the risk of instability and potentially even being overthrown. The risk of instability threatens the people of Europe even more than those of the US.

An end to Israel's occupation will immediately reduce tensions and instability in the region. The establishment of an independent Palestinian state and its normalization of relations with Israel as well as with surrounding Arab states will set the terms for the other Arab states' normalization of ties with Israel, further easing tensions in the Middle East. Certainly, many problems will remain; Israel's economy is many times larger than that of the surrounding Arab states, setting the threat of increasing inequity as the basis for regional economic cooperation. The "new Middle East" might look unfortunately similar to the "new North America," in which free trade agreements end up further enriching the US behemoth, while the much smaller Canadian and especially the far poorer Mexican economy pay the price.

But such developments are not inevitable. The potential remains for democratization and efforts for regional advancement as the trajectory of the next century. But all of that must wait until an end to Israel's occupation. And because anger at Israel's occupation translated so powerfully into anger toward the US, Israel's global patron, an end to occupation will also reduce antagonism toward US policies and indeed reduce the threat to ordinary Americans that those policies engender.

### Is a two-state arrangement fair and based on justice?

The search for justice means first acknowledging past injustices and then searching for how to establish just relations between people. Weighed according to the standard of absolute justice, creating a Palestinian state on only a small part of Palestine continues a historic injustice. Weighed according to UN resolutions and international law, establishing a Palestinian state on only 22 percent of the land, when the UN partition resolution designated 45 percent to become the Palestinian Arab state, is not really fair.

Throughout history, longstanding injustices sometimes become permanent. They do not become just or fair because time passes or power consolidates, but some of their results endure. The massive dispossession and genocide that led to the near-extermination of Native

Americans is no less unjust 400 years later. But while in 1607 it might have been legitimate to advocate the justice of sending all the European colonists back to Europe and returning all the land to the Native Americans, in 2007 the search for justice, while continuing, is very different. Human rights in the form of national recognition, treaty rights, economic reparations, affirmative action, protection of remaining tribal-held lands, and more are the new demands of Native Americans.

Certainly the Palestinian case is different. At the beginning of the 21st century, the Palestinian al-Nakba, or catastrophe, the 1948 war in which Palestinians were dispossessed from their land, was just over fifty years past. Many older Palestinians still remember fleeing their homes and still hold keys to the doors they have long imagined re-entering. Justice requires first that Israel acknowledge the truth of its responsibility for that dispossession and for denying the refugees their right to return. There must be an effort to recognize the legitimacy of international law, to restore lost lands and human rights, including the right of self determination.

The search for justice for Palestinians, so long denied their human and national rights, continues. The goals of ending occupation and establishing equal rights for all, based on international law and human rights, remain absolute. Many believe those goals can best be achieved through creation of an independent, viable, and sovereign State of Palestine in the West Bank, Gaza, and East Jerusalem. Such a solution—if based on the 1967 borders and including the complete withdrawal of soldiers and settlers not only from Palestinian territory but also from control over the new state's borders, realizing the right of return for Palestinian refugees, and ensuring equal rights and equal security for all Palestinians and Israelis both within and between the two states—would indeed be a huge accomplishment in the struggle for human rights and justice.

But as the construction of the Apartheid Wall and the continued expansion of the 440,000 settlers in huge city-sized settlements throughout the West Bank and East Jerusalem seem to make the creation of a viable Palestinian state impossible, more and more Palestinians are reconsidering the goal of creating a democratic secular or bi-national state in all of historic Palestine – encompassing what is now Israel, the West Bank, Gaza, and Jerusalem. Many, perhaps most Palestinians and at least a few Israelis, believe that over the long-term it is in the best interests of both peoples, even if there were an independent and sovereign Palestinian state, to create a single state, based on absolute equality for both nationalities and equal rights for all its citizens.

Certainly such an approach could only result from a free and open choice by both Israelis and Palestinians. Considering such an option is for the future; it will not likely reach the serious discussion stage until Israel and Palestine, and thus Israelis and Palestinians, can sit across a negotiating table as equals, not while they face each other, as today, as occupied and occupier. But the search for justice, in all its various forms, must continue.

# THE DIMINISHING LANDS OF PALESTINE

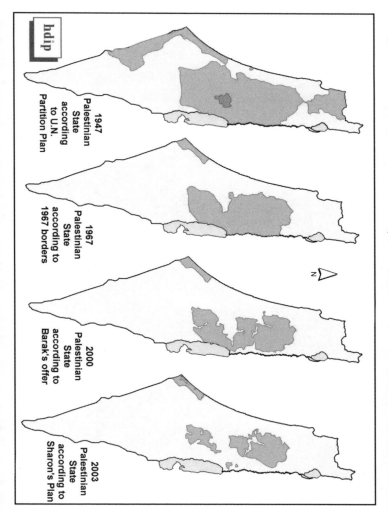

*Map courtesy of The Palestinian Health, Development, Information and Policy Organization (HDIP).*

# PART VI

# UPDATE TO THE THIRD EDITION: RECENT DEVELOPMENTS

## What happened at the 2007 Annapolis peace conference and how was it significant?

After several years of largely ignoring Israel–Palestine diplomatic efforts, the Bush administration suddenly pushed the issue to the front burner with the Annapolis peace conference in November 2007. The conference timing and agenda actually had far less to do with Israel–Palestine than with the Bush administration's need to rejuvenate flagging Arab government support for its failing war in Iraq and its intensifying mobili-zation against Iran.

The conference called for a two-state solution to be in place by the end of Bush's term. But immediately after, then Prime Minister Ehud Olmert stated Israel would not be bound by the new or even previous deadlines. Instead, his government announced the construction of hundreds of new homes in West Bank settlements.

The defiance worked. President Bush said nothing about the settlement expansion on his visit to the region shortly after the conference, and left office with US political and financial support for Israel's occupation policies intact.

## What is Iran's role in relation to Israel & the Palestinians?

During the years of the US-backed shah's regime (1953–1979), Israel and Iran developed close ties based on their centrality to US policy in the region and shared anti-Arab attitudes. Soon after the shah was ousted in 1979, relations between the two countries turned hostile. Throughout the George W. Bush administration, escalating US antagonism toward Iran strengthened the US–Israeli "special relationship." Tel Aviv and the pro-Israeli lobbies in the US strongly backed the US invasion of Iraq, but Israeli security officials and public opinion had long claimed that it was Iran that posed an "existential" threat to Israel.

In January 2007, Israeli Prime Minister Olmert threatened a possible military strike against Iran. Later that year Israel acknowledged purchasing 500 US-made bunker-buster bombs, aimed at destroying Iran's underground nuclear power facilities. In December, Israel rejected the US National Intelligence Estimate's conclusion that Iran did not have a nuclear weapons program. On June 6, 2008, the Israeli newspaper *Yedioth Ahronoth* quoted a government minister claiming that an Israeli attack with US support on Iranian nuclear sites was "unavoidable" because sanctions had failed. In February 2009 Israelis elected a right-wing government that continued threatening Iran.

In the United States, the intelligence community's increasing skepticism about Iran's alleged nuclear aspirations made a shift in the discourse possible. President Barack Obama has repeatedly indicated his openness to negotiations with Iran; in his June 2009 speech in Cairo, Obama stated his willingness to negotiate with Iran without preconditions and based on mutual respect.

Iran's support for Hamas (see page 62) is another factor in Israel's opposition. There is no question that Iran provides political support to Hamas; it is certainly likely that there has been financial support as well, and perhaps even some limited military support, although that remains unproven. However, Hamas is no puppet for Tehran and the level of Iranian support is often exaggerated.

### What were the reasons for and consequences of the Hamas–Fatah divide in 2007 and beyond?

From its origins, the Palestinian national movement has been composed of diverse, often-feuding factions. From the 1960s through the 1990s, the Palestine Liberation Organization, itself a coalition long dominated by the Fatah organization, was the centerpiece of Palestinian national life (see pages 33–35). Hamas, which emerged in Gaza in 1987 simultaneous with the first intifada, was never part of the historically secular PLO.

The PLO was ostensibly the official partner in negotiations with Israel and the US, but in fact it was largely sidelined by the Palestinian Authority, or PA, created in 1993 by the Oslo Accords. Until his 2004 death, Fatah leader Yasir Arafat served simultaneously as PLO chairman and PA president, as has his successor, Mahmoud Abbas. At least since 2000, Fatah has lost support as it failed to end the occupation and faced widespread accusations of corruption. The PLO's secular left parties have largely lost their vision and strategic direction and become less influential. Inside the occupied territories and among Palestinian refugees in the diaspora, new civil society organizations have begun setting national and global strategy, including the boycott, divestment, and sanctions program known as BDS. But the Fatah-led PLO–PA has still controlled Palestinian diplomacy, excluding both Hamas and much of civil society.

After Hamas won parliamentary elections in 2006, the Islamist organization formed a government dominated by independent technocrats. However, Israeli–US demonization and increasing Israeli repression made real governing power impossible. The Israeli–US position, backed by Europe, was to isolate the Palestinians, particularly Hamas, until they explicitly agreed to recognize Israel as a Jewish state, implement all earlier agreements, and renounce violence. There were no matching demands that Israel recognize a Palestinian state, abide by international laws and agreements, or cease its "targeted assassinations" in Gaza and military attacks in Gaza and the West Bank.

In February 2007, Palestinians formed a national unity government, but Fatah–Hamas tensions continued to mount. A short, brutal civil war broke out in June 2007, leading to the routing of Fatah supporters from Gaza, the dissolution of the unity government, and a greatly tightened boycott and Israeli siege of Hamas-controlled Gaza.

The Western media widely described this as a "Hamas coup," but the situation was much more complicated. *Vanity Fair* documented a covert action approved by President Bush and implemented by then Secretary of State Condoleezza Rice and Bush's Middle East advisor Elliott Abrams to provide millions of dollars of US weapons and military training to Fatah. When Congress balked at the spending, the Bush administration turned to key Arab allies for funds and weapons. In a confidential report, then UN representative to the so-called Quartet Alvaro de Soto stated that "the US clearly pushed for a confrontation between Fatah and Hamas." He added that the US envoy twice declared, "I like this violence."

Shortly after the Hamas victory, the Bush administration signed a 10-year, $30 billion military aid package for Israel, 75 percent of which would go to US arms dealers. President Obama agreed to implement the deal.

### What is the significance of Israel's siege and its 2008–2009 military attack on Gaza?

Immediately following Hamas's electoral victory in January 2006, Israel closed all borders with the Gaza Strip, despite the assessment of all European, US, and other international observers that the elections had been free and fair.

An Israeli wall encircles the entire Gaza Strip, with the Israeli military in complete control of the air space, coastal waters, and all border crossings including, indirectly, those into Egypt. Israel determines whether and how much food, fuel, parts for water treatment systems, medicine and medical equipment reach Gaza. Under the siege, the situation for Gaza's already-impoverished 1.5 million residents, 56 percent of whom are under the age of 18, became even more dire. In spring 2008 a coalition of British humanitarian agencies called the crisis "worse than at any time since the beginning of the Israeli military occupation in 1967." And that was *before* the military assault that began in December 2008.

Israel also continued its military raids, air strikes, and "targeted assassinations" in Gaza. The military wing of Hamas resumed rocket fire against Israel, in violation of the international laws governing the right to resist (which limit resistance to military targets, not civilians). Egypt took the lead in negotiating between Israel and Hamas, and in June 2008 a ceasefire was declared. For the next five months, the ceasefire largely held on the Palestinian side. As illustrated in a bar graph on the website of Israel's own Ministry of Foreign Affairs, earlier averages of up to 200 rockets per month dropped to an average of only two. During the periods of rocket fire, the residents of Sderot, the Israeli town nearest Gaza, were undoubtedly terrified—but not a single Israeli was injured or killed during the ceasefire. But during the ceasefire, Israeli forces killed at least 18 Palestinians in Gaza and broke their commitment to open border crossings.

On November 4, Israel effectively ended the ceasefire, killing six Palestinians in Gaza. The ceasefire officially expired December 26; Israeli air strikes and ground attacks in Gaza followed. Israeli officials claimed that the attack was an urgent response to the rocket fire. But the former Mossad head admitted that if protecting Israelis from rockets had really been the motivation, "opening the border crossings would have ensured such quiet for a generation." On December 31, senior Israeli defense officials admitted to *Ha'aretz* their government had "instructed the Israel Defense Forces to prepare for the operation over six months ago, even as Israel was beginning to negotiate a ceasefire agreement with Hamas." Rather than urgent necessity, the article identified "long-term preparation, careful gathering of information, secret discussions, operational deception and the misleading of the public" as the components of Israel's war strategy.

Israel's assault violated a range of international laws. According to the UN's Special Rapporteur on Human Rights in the Occupied Territories, Professor Richard Falk, the attack itself was illegal because Israel had a viable non-military alternative available to protect its people—returning to the ceasefire. The vastly disproportionate use of force was also illegal. According to the widely respected Palestinian Center for Human Rights in Gaza, during the 22 days of the assault, Israeli forces killed 1,417 Palestinians, of whom 926 were civilians, including 313 children and 116 women. Thirteen Israelis were killed, of whom three were civilians; four of the Israeli soldiers were killed by friendly fire. Israeli forces directly attacked individuals, some waving white flags, as well as schools, hospitals, mosques, and—in a separate violation—attacked UN facilities and personnel. Israel's use of collective punishment, penalizing 1.5 million civilians for the actions of a small group of militants, violated Article 33 of the Fourth Geneva Convention. And Israel's use of certain weapons—including white phosphorous bombs and flechette-filled bomblets—in civilian areas violated international prohibitions.

Israel's assault on Gaza could not have happened without Washington's direct support, including approximately $3 billion a year in military aid, plus parts for attack planes and helicopters, and additional weapons contracts. The assault violated the US Arms Export Control Act, which prohibits US arms from being used for any purpose other than security inside a country's borders or for legitimate self-defense purposes. Israel's attack did not meet those limitations, and the US government confirmed it was fully aware of Israel's plans before the assault.

The UN Security Council addressed the attack only reluctantly, and its resolution (with the US abstaining) was narrow and limited. The General Assembly's position, despite efforts by GA President Father Miguel d'Escoto and others to pass a much stronger resolution, echoed the weak Security Council approach. By using or threatening its veto and other pressures to protect Israel from being held accountable in the United Nations, the US was also indirectly complicit in Israeli violations.

***What happened in the February 2009 Israeli elections?***
All of the top candidates for prime minister—Foreign Minister Tsipi Livni of the centrist Kadima Party, Benjamin Netanyahu of the right-wing Likud, and Defense Minister Ehud Barack of the center-left Labor Party—backed the Gaza assault, which Israeli Jews across the political spectrum had over-whelmingly supported.

Likud and Kadima came in virtually neck-and-neck. The Labor Party, for generations the most influential force in Israeli politics, was a weak fourth. Third place went to the far-right racist party Yisrael Beiteinu, whose leader Avigdor Lieberman (see pages 58–59) was appointed foreign minister. Lieberman has called for forcing Palestinian citizens to swear loyalty to Israel as an exclusively Jewish state, drowning Palestinian prisoners held by Israel, and executing Palestinian members of the Knesset who meet with Hamas. While some Israeli leaders repudiated Lieberman's most extreme statements, the election consolidated explicitly racist politics at the center of Israel's mainstream.

Netanyahu is the first post-Oslo Israeli prime minister to officially reject the "two-state solution"—although every prime minister before him had carried out policies that made a real two-state solution impossible. Responding to President Obama, Netanyahu used the words "Palestinian state" in a June 2009 speech, but reiterated Israel's longstanding rejection of real Palestinian statehood, independence, sovereignty, and self-determination. He demanded Palestinian recognition and acceptance of Israel as the "national homeland of the Jewish People," not a state of all its citizens, thus requiring Palestinians to accept the legitimacy of Israel's discriminatory practices, denied the right of return, and made no mention of the devastated Gaza Strip.

### What are the new possibilities and new challenges facing US policy on Israel–Palestine under President Barack Obama?

The 2007–2008 US presidential campaign took place during a period of profound shifts in US discourse regarding the Israeli–Palestinian conflict. New Jewish anti-occupation organizations emerged, and US civil society organizations embraced the 2005 call from their Palestinian and global counterparts to support boycotts, divestment, and sanctions to nonviolently challenge Israeli occupation and apartheid. The use of the term "apartheid" to describe Israeli policies of discrimination, dispossession, and separation became commonplace, aided by President Jimmy Carter's 2007 book *Palestine: Peace Not Apartheid*. Palestinian voices were prominent in media coverage and events commemorating the 40th anniversary of the 1967 war and occupation and the 60th anniversary of the *nakba*, the 1948 Palestinian dispossession.

Early in Barack Obama's campaign, he made the notable remark that "no one has suffered as much as the Palestinians." However, most of his campaign rhetoric did not significantly diverge from a boilerplate pro-Israeli stance. Since his election, Obama's messages have been mixed. He remained mute during the Israeli assault on Gaza, and soon after taking office, he re-affirmed President Bush's commitment to provide $30 billion in military aid to Israel over the next ten years.

On the other hand, Obama stated unequivocally that the Israeli–Palestinian conflict should be removed from the "global war on terror" framework. Rather than choosing a pro-Israel hardliner for special envoy, he chose former senator George Mitchell, whose 2001 fact-finding delegation targeted the dangers posed by Jewish settlements in the occupied territories. In his Cairo speech in June 2009, Obama said the US "does not accept" the legitimacy of continued Israeli settlements, and "it is time for these settlements to stop." Early indications also hint at a willingness to engage with Hamas, a crucial shift in US policy.

As of June 2009, it remains unclear whether President Obama will be willing to back up his strong language with the tough pressure needed to achieve his goal of a two-state solution. That would require withholding military aid to Israel, conditioning the aid on an immediate and complete settlement freeze as a modest first step. Netanyahu's blatant rejectionism could make it easier for Obama to take tough action. Less combative Israeli leaders have muddied the diplomatic waters by talking of "two states" and "dismantling outposts," while consolidating occupation, building settlements and walls of separation, seizing

Palestinian land and dividing what remains into non-contiguous cantons, increasing what Israelis themselves call the Judaization of Arab East Jerusalem, and maintaining a lethal siege on the Gaza Strip.

For those working for peace and justice in Israel and Palestine, the challenge remains to transform the changing discourse into real US policy change.

# RESOURCES

### Books

Abunimah, Ali. *One Country: A Bold Proposal to End the Israeli–Palestinian Impasse*. New York: Metropolitan Books, 2007.

Aruri, Naseer. *Dishonest Broker: The US Role in Israel and Palestine*. Cambridge, Mass.: South End Press, 2003.

———. *Palestinian Refugees: The Right of Return*. London: Pluto Press, 2001.

Asali, K.J. *Jerusalem in History*. Northampton, Mass.: Olive Branch Press, 1999.

Beit-Hallahmi, Benjamin. *Original Sins: Reflections on the History of Zionism and Israel*. Northampton, Mass.: Olive Branch Press, 1998.

Bennis, Phyllis. *Before and After: US Foreign Policy and the War on Terrorism*. 2nd ed. Northampton, Mass.: Olive Branch Press, 2003.

———. *Calling the Shots: How Washington Dominates Today's UN*. Northampton, Mass.: Olive Branch Press, 2000.

Boullata, Kamal, and Kathy Engel, eds. *We Begin Here: Poems for Palestine and Lebanon*. Northampton, Mass.: Olive Branch Press, 2007.

Carter, Jimmy. *Palestine: Peace Not Apartheid*. New York: Simon and Schuster, 2007.

Chomsky, Noam. *The Fateful Triangle: The United States, Israel and the Palestinians*. Cambridge, Mass.: South End Press, 1999.

Falk, Richard. *Unlocking the Middle East: The Writings of Richard Falk*. Ed. Jean Allain. Northampton, Mass.: Olive Branch Press, 2002.

Farsoun, Samih, and Naseer Aruri. *Palestine and the Palestinians: A Social and Political History*. 2nd ed. Boulder: Westview Press, 2006.

Finkelstein, Norman. *Beyond Chutzpah: On the Misuse of Anti-Semitism and the Abuse of History*. Berkeley: University of California Press, 2005.

Hadawi, Sami. *Bitter Harvest: A Modern History of Palestine*. 4th ed. Northampton, Mass.: Olive Branch Press, 1998.

Halper, Jeff. *An Israeli In Palestine: Resisting Dispossession, Redeeming Israel*. London: Pluto Press, 2008.

Hass, Amira. *Drinking the Sea at Gaza: Days and Nights in a Land Under Siege*. New York: Henry Holt, 2000.

Hiro, Dilip. *Sharing the Promised Land: A Tale of Israelis and Palestinians*. Northampton, Mass.: Olive Branch Press, 1999.

Khalidi, Rashid. *Palestinian Identity: The Construction of Modern National Consciousness*. New York: Columbia University Press, 1998.

————. *The Iron Cage: The Story of the Palestinian Struggle for Statehood*. Boston: Beacon Press, 2006.

Khalidi, Walid. *Before Their Diaspora: A Photographic History of the Palestinians 1876–1948*. Washington, DC: Institute for Palestine Studies, 2004.

————. *All That Remains: The Palestinian Villages Occupied and Depopulated by Israel in 1948*. Washington, DC: Institute for Palestine Studies, 1992.

————. *From Haven to Conquest: Readings in Zionism and the Palestine Problem until 1948*. Washington, DC: Institute for Palestine Studies, 1987.

Masalha, Nur. *Imperial Israel and the Palestinians: The Politics of Expansion*. London: Pluto Press, 2000.

Massoulie, Francois. *Middle East Conflicts: An Illustrated History*. Northampton, Mass.: Olive Branch Press, 1998.

McGeough, Paul. *Kill Khalid: The Failed Mossad Assassination of Khalid Mishal and the Rise of Hamas*. New York: The New Press, 2009.

McGowan, Dan, and Marc Ellis. *Remembering DeirYassin: The Future of Israel and Palestine*. Northampton, Mass.: Olive Branch Press, 1998.

Mearsheimer, John, and Stephen Walt. *The Israel Lobby and US Foreign Policy*. New York: Farrar, Straus and Giroux, 2007.

Mishal, Shaul, and Azraham Sela. *The Palestinian Hamas*. 2nd ed. New York: Columbia University Press, 2006.

Pappe, Ilan. *The Ethnic Cleansing of Palestine*. London: Oneworld Publications, 2007.

Prior, Michael, ed. *Speaking the Truth: Zionism, Israel and Occupation*. Northampton, Mass.: Olive Branch Press, 2004.

Rogan, Eugene, and Avi Shlaim. *The War for Palestine: Rewriting the History of 1948*. 2nd ed. Cambridge, Mass.: Cambridge University Press, 2007.

Roy, Sara. *The Gaza Strip: The Political Economy of De-Development*. Washington, DC: Institute for Palestine Studies, 1995.

Rubenberg, Cheryl. *The Palestinians: In Search of A Just Peace*. Boulder: Lynne Rienner, 2003.

————. *Palestinian Women: Patriarchy and Resistance in the West Bank*. Boulder: Lynne Rienner, 2001.

Said, Edward W. *The Question of Palestine*. 2nd ed. New York: Vintage Books, 1992.

————. *Peace and its Discontents: Essays on Palestine in the Middle East Peace Process*. New York: Vintage Books, 1996.

————. *The End of the Peace Process: Oslo and After*. New York: Vintage Books, 2001.

Schleifer, Abdullah. *The Fall of Jerusalem*. New York: Monthly Review Press, 1972.

Shahin, Mariam. *Palestine: A Guide*. Photography by George Azar. Northampton, Mass.: Interlink Books, 2006.

Suleiman, Michael W. *US Policy on Palestine: From Wilson to Clinton*. Washington, DC: Association of Arab-American University Graduates, 1994.

Swisher, Clayton E. *The Truth About Camp David*. New York: Nation Books, 2004.

Tamimi, Azzam. *Hamas: A History from Within*. Northampton, Mass.: Olive Branch Press, 2007.

Usher, Graham. *Dispatches From Palestine: The Rise and Fall of the Oslo Peace Process*. London: Pluto Press, 1999.

Warschawski, Michel. *On the Border*. Cambridge, Mass.: South End Press, 2004.

Zertal, Idith, and Akiva Eldar. *Lords of the Land: The War for Israel's Settlements in the Occupied Territories 1967–2007*. New York: Nation Books, 2007.

## *Organizations in the US*
### American-Arab Anti-Discrimination Committee
Supports Palestinian rights and challenges anti-Arab racism in the US. www.adc.org

### Americans for Middle East Understanding
Founded 34 years ago by Americans whose professions in medicine, church ministry, archaeology and diplomacy had taken them to the Middle East. Publishes *The Link* on a bimonthly basis and sponsors educational programs. www.ameu.org

### American Friends Service Committee
This Quaker educational organization provides resources, talking points, and educational materials. www.afsc.org

### Electronic Intifada
Launched in February 2001; challenges myth, distortion, and spin in the media coverage of the Palestinians and the Israeli–Palestinian Conflict. www.electronicintifada.net

### Foundation for Middle East Peace
Publishes a bimonthly report on Israeli settlements in the occupied territories. www.fmep.org

### Institute for Middle East Understanding
Places relevant op-eds in mainstream news outlets, and makes Palestinian voices accessible to US and international journalists. www.imeu.org

### Institute for Palestine Studies
Publishes the *Journal of Palestine Studies*, the *Jerusalem Quarterly*, and a wide variety of books and other materials in English, French, and Arabic. www.ipsjps.org

### Jewish Voice for Peace
One of the leading Jewish anti-occupation organizations working inside the Jewish community and in broader coalitions.
www.jewishvoiceforpeace.org

### J-Street
A lobby that defines itself as the "political arm of the pro-Israel, pro-peace" movement. www.jstreet.org

### Middle East Children's Alliance
Supports children's projects in the occupied territories and provides educational resources in the US on human rights and peace and justice issues. www.mecaforpeace.org

### Middle East Research and Information Project (MERIP)
An independent think tank in Washington, DC, and publisher of the *Middle East Report*, a quarterly magazine with critical analysis of current issues in the Middle East. Also produces MER Online. www.merip.org

**Palestine Center**
The educational arm of the Washington-based Jerusalem fund.
www.palestinecenter.org

**Rachel Corrie Foundation for Peace and Justice**
Works to support people in the Gaza Strip.
www.rachelcorriefoundation.org

**Sabeel**
An ecumenical center in Jerusalem for Palestinian Liberation
Theology. Friends of Sabeel North America holds conferences across
the US. www.sabeel.org

**Trans-Arab Research Institute**
www.tari.org

**US Campaign to End the Israeli Occupation**
The largest US coalition on the issue, with almost 300 member
organizations. Works toward an end to the occupation and equal
rights for all, and a US Middle East policy based on human rights,
international law, and UN resolutions. www.endtheoccupation.org

*Organizations in the Region*
**Adalah**
The legal center for Arab minority rights in Israel. www.adalah.org

**Alternative Information Center**
A joint Palestinian—Israeli organization that provides information,
political advocacy, grassroots activism, and critical analysis.
www.alternativenews.org

**Badil Resource Center for Palestinian Refugee &
Residency Rights**
Provides resources and information on the Palestinian refugees to
achieve a just and lasting solution based on the right of return.
www.badil.org

**Bat Shalom**
An Israeli women's organization that advocates peace and justice
between Israelis and Palestinians and women's rights. Conducts